The Politics of New Media Theatre

The Politics of New Media Theatre is a groundbreaking study of performance that responds to, adopts and subverts current philosophical, political and economic practices. Not only does Gabriella Giannachi show how new media theatre can affect society, she also demonstrates that knowledge produced by and through performance is paradigmatic towards an understanding of the contemporary. In doing this the book addresses such questions as:

- What is the role of theatre within globalisation?
- Can branding and patenting be affected by performance?
- What happens when life itself becomes a registered trademark?
- How can performativity subvert productivity?
- What is post-human performance?
- What do science and theatre have in common?

An interdisciplinary study, this book covers many fields including performance, digital art, recombinant theatre, hacktivism, globalisation, surveillance, cloning, genomics, architecture, corporate business, new media, body art, prank, bioart, Artificial Intelligence and Artificial Life, robotics, semi-living art, xenotransplantation, cellular practice and swarming.

This outstanding new work offers an analysis of leading political, philosophical and artistic texts and artworks, and represents a milestone for anyone interested in new technologies, theatre and politics.

Gabriella Giannachi is Senior Lecturer in Drama and Co-director of the Centre for Intermedia at the University of Exeter, UK. Her books include: *On Directing* (with M. Luckhurst, 1999), *Staging the Post-Avant-Garde* (with N. Kaye, 2002), *Virtual Theatres* (2004) and *Performing Nature* (with N. Stewart, 2005). She is a Co-Investigator of the AHRC-funded 'Performing Presence' project (Exeter University, University College London and Stanford University).

Routledge advances in theatre and performance studies

The Politics of New Media Theatre

Life®™

Gabriella Giannachi

The Politics of New Media Theatre: Life®™
is supported by

Routledge
Taylor & Francis Group

LONDON AND NEW YORK

Arts & Humanities
Research Council

First published 2007
by Routledge
2 Park Square, Milton Park, Abingdon, Oxon OX14 4RN

Simultaneously published in the USA and Canada
by Routledge
270 Madison Ave, New York, NY 10016

Routledge is an imprint of the Taylor & Francis Group, an informa business

Transferred to Digital Printing 2009

© 2007 Gabriella Giannachi

Typeset in Garamond by Wearset Ltd, Boldon, Tyne and Wear

British Library Cataloguing in Publication Data
A catalogue record for this book is available from the British Library

Library of Congress Cataloging in Publication Data
A catalog record for this book has been requested

ISBN10: 0–415–34946–X (hbk)
ISBN10: 0–415–54409–2 (pbk)
ISBN10: 0–203–69514–3 (ebk)

ISBN13: 978–0–415–34946–8 (hbk)
ISBN13: 978–0–415–54409–2 (pbk)
ISBN13: 978–0–203–69514–2 (ebk)

To Barbara Lanati
and to the memory of Tony Tanner
with gratitude

Contents

Illustrations

Acknowledgements

This project has received significant institutional support that has been essential to its completion. I would like to thank the Arts and Humanities Research Council for offering financial assistance for research travel to essential archives and sites in Italy, Germany and the UK. I am also indebted to Keith Stringer and the Research Committee of Lancaster University for supporting this project at its inception and to the University of Exeter and my colleagues in the Department of Drama for providing additional support to the project through an important period of sabbatical leave. I am also grateful to Exeter University for assistance with respect to the publication of some of the images reproduced in this book. In addition, I am indebted to my colleagues at Exeter for a friendly, stimulating and supportive research environment.

My former colleagues Wallace Heim, Kate Newey and Andrew Quick furnished expertise regarding various parts of the project. Michael Shanks at Stanford University offered, at different points in time, thought-provoking comments on the subject at large, which influenced much more than just the writing of specific sections of this book. I would also like to thank Steve Kurtz, Stelarc, Matt Adams and Blast Theory for important interview materials and Jonathan Slack, Karl Sims, The Yes Men and ®TMark, Bill Brown from Surveillance Camera Players, etoy, Matt Adams, Oron Catts and Ionat Zurr from SymbioticA for email exchanges clarifying aspects of their work. I am also grateful to my students for new and refreshing insight and dedication to the subject, and, last but not least, to Talia Rodgers, Joe Whiting and Terry Clague from Routledge for commissioning the book and seeing it to completion.

The artists and scientists in this book have been wonderfully helpful and extremely generous in providing materials, offering comments and overall feedback. This book would not be the same without their passion, originality, commitment, aesthetic, scientific and political insight. To them we all owe a considerable debt.

For encouragement and advice I would also, as always, like to thank my parents who, despite much adversity, are still finding the time and energy to be at my side, and my husband and daughter, for being there when it mattered most. I am particularly indebted to Nick Kaye for his unfailing support and enthusiasm, and for commenting intelligently draft after draft, on all aspects of this project. I am, of course, also indebted to my three-year-old daughter Francesca whose love, warmth and energy always make such a difference.

This book is dedicated to Barbara Lanati, whose witty and illuminating lectures about American literature, art, film, theatre and life, and whose enduring commitment and dedication to students, persistence and patience in dealing with unfathomable bureaucracy, are still a model for me today.

This book is also dedicated to the memory of Tony Tanner for his acumen, energy, friendship, curiosity and phenomenal support throughout the years, and for his absolute passion for knowledge, which makes him still such a major inspiration today. He is very much missed.

I am grateful to Routledge and the editors of *Contemporary Theatre Review* for permission to reproduce sections of 'Global' and 'Cell' that previously appeared in *Contemporary Theatre Review*, Special Issue: Theatre and Globalisation, 16.1 (February 2006). I am also pleased to acknowledge the kind permission of the following individuals and companies to reproduce the illustrations that make such a crucial contribution to this volume: Ricardo Dominguez and Electronic Disturbance Theater, The Yes Men with ®TMark, etoy, Marcel.lí Antúnez Roca, Christa Sommerer and Laurent Mignonneau, 0100101110101101.ORG, the Roslin Institute, Ionat Zurr and Oron Catts from SymbioticA, Matt Adams and Blast Theory, Steve Kurtz and Critical Art Ensemble, Surveillance Camera Players, Stelarc, Thomas Ray, Eduardo Kac, Ken Goldberg, Char Davies, Kevin Warwick, Knowbotic Research and Karl Sims.

1 Introduction

Ours is a world that ventures blindly into the new with its fingers crossed.
(Wark, 2004: 001)

The Politics of New Media Theatre: Life®™ offers the reader a series of lenses focused on different but interrelated spheres of nature and society. The direction is that of a descent, from global to city, from body to animals, plants, and, finally, cells. The fact that there is a descent is, however, not metaphorical of a fall. Quite the contrary, this book suggests that the solution to the global concerns of our times can be found in and through cellular models.

The book begins with a study of globalisation, the largest and most comprehensive filter through which to analyse the contemporary. Globalisation is treated here not only as a phase in the development of capitalism but as a framework for social, political and cultural life. Globalisation operates primarily at the level of information. This is the first thesis of the book, that *the information society performs globalisation*.

The spectacle of globalisation is generated in and by our 'global' cities, acting as broadcasters of information, always monitoring, informing, disseminating, connecting different world g(l)ocalities. By observing the ways in which global cities layer facts and fictions, façades and screens, space and place, we may not only witness how globalisation continuously reconstitutes itself as a hybrid of materiality and virtuality, product and brand, live and mediated, but also see how we ourselves continuously operate in these tensions. Thus the second thesis of the book is that because fictions, as well as facts, determine our economic, political and cultural performance, *the politics of information is also an aesthetics*.

Where the principal producer of globalisation is the global city region, the most significant sphere within which globalisation operates is that of the body. Following the decoding of the human genome, the body, whether human or animal, is increasingly equated to and treated as information. Because of this, the body is not only post-human but also trans-human. Part animal, part plant, part object, this body becomes at once an instrument and a producer of globalisation. Thus the third thesis of this book is that *the interconnected, networked, post-human body is both the industry that produces globalisation as well as its principal consumer.*

The fundamental level at which globalisation operates on the body is cellular. It is at this level, at the level of molecules and particles, that it determines what and who we are. But the cell is not only the principal means by which globalisation intervenes onto the body, it is also the fundamental site from which to operate an info-politics. It is crucial that info-politics absorbs a biopolitics so that the ongoing transformation of life into life®™ is a democratic, open and an internationally lawful process. Cellular practice is where information and politics coincide. The fourth thesis of this volume is that *cellular practice is at the heart of info-politics.*

The Politics of New Media Theatre: Life®™ rests on three fundamental axioms. The first one is that *technology is material, literary and social.* This axiom is derived from the seminal study *Leviathan and the Air-Pump* (1989; [1985]), where Steven Shapin and Simon Schaffer, with reference to Robert Boyle's air-pump, demonstrate that there are three technologies: *a material technology*, 'embedded in the construction and operation of the air-pump'; *a literary technology*, 'by means of which the phenomena produced by the pump were made known to those who were not direct witnesses'; and *a social technology*, 'that incorporated the conventions experimental philosophers should use in dealing with each other and considering knowledge-claims'. Literary and social practices, Shapin and Schaffer demonstrate, as well as machines, 'are *knowledge-producing tools*' (ibid.: 25, added emphasis). Each of these incorporates the others. This means that technology, culture and society do not operate separately but are intrinsically embedded in one another. Technology is not only grounded in materiality but also in discourse, fiction and society. By dislodging technology at the material and literary levels, the artists described in this monograph are therefore able to effect technology as a means of social and political interaction.

The second axiom at the heart of this book is that *artistic performance impacts on economic performance.* This position is derived from Jon McKenzie's fascinating *Perform or Else* (2001) in which the author draws attention to the utilisation of the concept and practice of performance in management, art and technological innovation. In his study, McKenzie argues that performance is 'an onto-historical formation of power and knowledge' (ibid.: 194) and that 'individuals work and live only to enact performances dictated by others, performances normalized according to the dictates of expediency and efficiency' (ibid.: 160). Performance, McKenzie suggests, 'functions as a formation of power: as a mode of domination', the performance principle therefore 'extends a certain technological rationality and economic alienation into all social organizations and, through mass culture, into leisure activities and private life' (ibid.: 161). Within this framework the 'power of performance operates through social stratifications such as gender, sexual, ethnic, racial, class, and religious identity, where blocks of performatives and performances constitute different subject positions within different language games' (ibid.: 181). By operating through performance, the practices presented in this book function at a 'nonreproductive', ontologically unstable level (see Phelan, 1993: 148). This suggests that within performance there is a non-necessary, non-reproducible, flickering *surplus* which, however unstable, can effect real social and political change precisely because of this ontological hybridity.

This position, after Peggy Phelan's *Unmarked: The Politics of Performance* (1993), is also inspired by Guy Debord's *The Society of the Spectacle* (1995; [1967]) in which the author claims that '[t]he whole life of those societies in which modern conditions of production prevail presents itself as *an immense accumulation of spectacles*. All that once was directly lived has become mere representation' (ibid.: 12, added emphasis). The spectacle, Debord suggests, 'is *capital* accumulated to the point where it becomes image' (ibid.: 24, original emphasis); 'it is the world of commodity ruling over all lived experience' (ibid.: 26) so that 'commodities are now *all* that there is to see' (ibid.: 29, original emphasis). *At the level of the spectacle, the world of art and that of economics resolve into one another causing an excess, capital or surplus of information. This excess is where art is politically and aesthetically charged.*

The third axiom of this book is written after Nick Kaye's influential *Site-Specific Art* (2000). Here Kaye argues that site-specificity

> arises in a disturbance of the opposition between 'virtual' and 'real' spaces, in a dialectical relationship between the work and its site, or in a questioning of the art object's material integrity, so the very possibility of establishing a work's proper location is called into question.
>
> (ibid.: 183)

The site-specificity of the practices presented in his book, Kaye notes, 'arises precisely in uncertainties over the borders and limits of work and site' (ibid.: 215). *The Politics of New Media Theatre: Life*®™ consists of a series of explorations of multiple and dislocated practices and knowledges. These are overlaid by one another, creating imperfect but on occasion cumulative intertextualities. The superimposition intends to identify excesses, capitals, as well as zones of difference. Thus the dislocative, multiple, fragmented, ambivalent and especially *uncertain* qualities of the aesthetics presented in this study constitute the unstable grounds within which processes of *Verfremdung* rather than of *Entfremdung* are allowed to occur. These are the sites for a post-modern politics. Thus the third axiom of the book is that *uncertainty is at the root of the politics of knowledge*.

The Politics of New Media Theatre: Life®™ was written in the attempt to engage with a number of seemingly irreconcilable tensions. These tensions map over the two fundamental fields that I discuss in this study, namely nature and society. These two fields are of course profoundly embedded in one another and in many ways this book represents an attempt to argue that only at the levels of nature *and* society can politics have a longlasting and global impact.

The first tension explored in this book is that between ecology and post-modern cultural history. According to ecology, nature is an objective and tangible reality that urgently needs to be safeguarded from destabilising human intervention. According to post-modern cultural history, nature is a cultural construction whose definition and parameters vary through history and geographical boundaries. According to ecology, nature needs preservation. According to cultural history, nature, by definition, implies change. According to ecology there are effective strategies that must be employed in order to maintain nature 'as it is'. According to cultural history, the concept and practice of nature develop with and through progress to include what in its original definition it was not – the technological, the genetically modified, the other. But where does this leave an ecological practice that also has a post-modern cultural history? What of ecological ethics *and* post-modern cultural discourse?

As suggested in the introduction to *Futurenatural* (1996), the concept of nature is fragile and unstable precisely because it is a 'product of discourse' while its referent represents a 'subject of politics' (Robertson *et al.*, 1996: 1). Nature resides both in discourse *and* in practice. It can be both conceptualised *and* performed (see Szerszynski *et al.*, 2003; and Giannachi and Stewart, 2005). While, as in Kate Soper's words, nature is being constituted 'in the chain of the signifier', it also represents the 'independent domain of intrinsic value, truth or authenticity' (in Robertson *et al.*, 1996: 22) that is at the heart of the political debate around ecological and environmental welfare. This means that nature must be read as both post-cultural and non-cultural, as both the product of discourse and what is as yet outside it. Because nature, including technologically reproduced nature, is in discourse, by performing at the level of the sign, of information, it is possible to modify the economic and biological performances of nature. This position allows for an ecological *and* post-modern politics of nature that affects not only nature but also discourse, again, technologically, literarily and socially. For this position I am of course indebted to Bruno Latour's decisive findings in *Politics of Nature* (2004), which suggest the possibility of a *multi-naturalism* in which the theatres of *nature and society are no longer separate.*

The second tension explored owes much to Umberto Eco's *Apocalittici e Integrati* (1964), and deals with the construction of *societas* within nature. The focus here is on the collapse of history, politics and form out of which a new biotechnologically assisted 'nature' is emerging. Jean Baudrillard claims that 'in the case of the Gulf War as in the case of the events in Eastern Europe, we are no longer dealing with "historical events" but with places of collapse' (1995: 70). This collapse, of nation states, ideologies, welfare systems, society, party politics, artistic form and content, is an unquestionable feature of our age. Yet out of this collapse, of the ruins of our history, new structures are emerging. So while Francis Fukuyama famously called for

The End of History (1992), barely a decade later he himself was forced to revisit his provocative claim to argue that biotechnology, the very science through which it is possible to recombine, engineer and manipulate DNA and other molecules, currently produces such tangible effects for world politics (2002: 19) that history can no longer be considered dead. Arguing now that as long as there is science there is history (ibid.: xi ff.), Fukuyama identifies 'social control' (ibid.: 53) as a determining factor in contemporary politics and predicts that genetic inequality will become 'one of the chief controversies of twenty-first century politics' (ibid.: 160). His question: '[w]hat will happen to political rights once we are able to, in effect, breed some people with saddles on their backs, and others with boots and spurs?' (ibid.: 10) is of crucial consequence to the thinking behind this book. *The societas of nature, inclusive of human, trans-human and non-human beings, must become the theatre of info-politics.*

Far from witnessing the end of history, and therewith, the end of politics, I note what has been described as the growing politicisation of the *homo economicus* (Rosenkrands in van de Donk *et al.*, 2004: 59). This politicisation is a necessary consequence to the growing influence that this *homo economicus*, the finest product of capitalist evolution, now has over nature and society. Jeremy Rifkin is a point of influence here. Rifkin observes the necessity for a powerful and new social and political current: '[a]t the epicentre is a technology revolution unmatched in all of history in its power to make ourselves, our institutions, and our world.' Here Rifkin identifies technology, in all its complex ramifications, as responsible for the fundamental changes to society and nature that define our age. 'Before our eyes', Rifkin proposes, 'lies an uncharted new landscape whose contours are being shaped in thousands of biotechnology laboratories in universities, government agencies, and corporations around the world.' The consequences of these changes, Rifkin concludes, 'for society and future generations are likely to be enormous' (1998: 1). This analysis is crucial. Although technology operates at the level of the modification, augmentation and virtualisation of the real, its most significant and disturbing effect manifests itself at the level of nature. Within the information society, it is the nature of society as well as the *societas* of nature that is at stake.

Rifkin shows how a 'handful of global corporations, research institutions, and governments could hold patents on virtually all 100,000 genes that make up the blueprints of the human race, as well as the cells, organs, and tissues that comprise the human body'. 'They also', he notes, 'own similar patents on tens of thousands of micro-organisms, plants, and animals, allowing them unprecedented power to dictate the terms by which we and future generations will live our lives' (ibid.: 2). This marks the beginning of an era in which we will witness the exploitation of genetic resources for specific economic ends, the awarding of patents as an incentive to the marketplace for the exploitation of these resources, 'the wholesale reseeding of the earth's biosphere with a laboratory-conceived second Genesis', the 'wholesale alteration of the human species and the birth of a commercially driven eugenics civilization' (ibid.: 8–9). This also marks the necessity of a bio-political info-politics in which through the 'performance' of technology we can change society. This is where I depart from Rifkin. The fact that techno-logy now allows us to more substantially rewrite life itself is a fundamental milestone for civilisation. It is up to us to make it our *genesis* rather than apocalypse.

While Rifkin identifies the biotechnological revolution with awful and terrifying visions of trans-human slavery, in which we will witness an unprecedented exploitation of the planet and a rewriting of the very nature of society, Antonio Negri salutes biopolitics as the space 'within which rela-tions, fights and productions of power are developed' (2003: 82). This allows me to introduce the third and final tension explored in this book. This is between science and theatre arts. I claim here, that the answer to many scientific questions, concerns and fears lies in the *modus operandi* of art and vice versa, that art and aesthetics inform and promulgate scientific innova-tion. Theatre has always been part of the way science operates, so much so that we talk of theatres of science throughout modern history. Science, of course, has time and again constituted a fundamental model for theatre, so much so that we talk of laboratories and studies when trying to capture the way by which artists prepare or rehearse their work. In *The Politics of New Media Theatre: Life*®™ I present the work of scientists alongside that of artists precisely because I believe that the most interesting and longlasting politics of the twenty-first century will emerge out of the collaboration between art and science.

Eugene Thacker identifies biomedia as 'novel configurations of biologies and technologies that take us beyond the familiar tropes of technology-as-tool or the human–machine interface.' (2004: 6). Biomedia, Thacker intelli-gently shows, surpass the tensions between culture and nature, biology and technology, information and life. In both Negri's and Thacker's analyses, it is clear that the biological and the digital domains are no longer distinct but 'inherent' in one another, so that 'the biological "informs" the digital, just as the digital "corporealizes" the biological' (ibid.: 7). At the heart of the glob-alisation of the biotechnological industry is therefore the very 'integration between biology and informatics, genetic and computer "codes"' (ibid.: 47). This suggests that there is contamination between the processes, modes and technologies of information that constitute art and science, technology and biology, nature, culture and society, locality and globalisation, individual and mass, and it is precisely at the level of this contamination, of this hybridity, or excess, that the info-politics produced by the re-evolutionary coming together of art, economics and science can produce social and polit-ical change.

2   Global

In many ways this war on terror is a war about information.
If we have information we can defeat the enemy.
(attorney general nominee Senator Alberto Gonzalez, 6 January 2005)

Performing globalisation

In economic terms globalisation indicates a phase in the development of capitalism (Lash and Urry, 1987, 1994). One of the principal characteristics of this phase is that it signals a movement beyond the nation state (Giddens, 1990; Beck, 2000; Hardt and Negri, 2000) in which the nation state is not only replaced politically and economically, but also 'as the decisive framework for social life' (Featherstone and Lash, 1995: 2). The vacuum left by the economical and political 'dis-appearance' of the nation state and the subsequent deregulation (and de-nationalisation) of state-owned services has been affecting not only the way we understand and make politics, the manner in which we work or even think of our 'productivity' and 'performance', but also the very way we live our lives, eat, drink, conceive and educate our children, deal with pleasure and illness, die. Globalisation is both global in that it attempts to affect 'everybody' in the world *and* in that it concerns all the strata of our lives. Not only does it designate the fading of the sovereignty of the nation state, and so to a certain extent the end of democracy, but it also tells us that this phenomenon somehow involves the entire world population, regardless of race, gender, socio-political background and religion.

Globalisation indicates, very much like post-modernism, a condition, an inescapable structure of feeling, able to portray both the economic, political and sociological parameters that have been manifesting themselves since the latter part of the twentieth century, as well as rendering the predominant artistic and philosophical concerns of the 'cultural logic of late capitalism' (Jameson, 1991). Described as 'an irresistible force of nature, as much outside our influence as the weather' (Giddens, 2000: 12), globalisation designates both an economic and political 'reality', as well as a sociological, philosophical and cultural *Weltanschauung*. This semiotic ambiguity is reflected in the wealth of its definitions, so that while it is depicted as unavoidable (Beck, 2000), the very consequence of modernity (Giddens, 1990), it is also presented as structural (Chase-Dunn *et al.*, 2000), or even performed (Franklin *et al.*, 2000). Hence while globalisation is structurally *there* for all of us to experience, it is actually primarily encountered in and through its 'performance'. Our politics *act out* global aims, our markets *perform* globally, our social, philosophical and aesthetic vocabularies are increasingly being *practised* under the influence of global tendencies. Whether individually, through what we eat, drink, wear, or as a social group, through our employers, schools, states, we are all participating in the practice of globalisation.

So what is it that we are performing in? What does globalisation stand for? In her study of this phenomenon, Celia Lury defines a brand as 'a set of relations between products or services'. A brand, she emphasises, has certain qualities: it is incorporeal, intangible, not fixed in time and space in terms of presence and absence and yet 'it is a mode of organising activities in time and space'. A brand is not here or there but it 'emerges in parts', implicates social relations, and is 'identifiable in its doing' (2004: 1). Acknowledging her debt to Lev Manovich's description of the new media object (2001), Lury describes the brand as comprising a '*dynamic platform or support for practice*' (2004: 6, original emphasis). Thus the brand, she notes, 'is not simply a machine for the production or consumption of information; it retains margins of indeterminacy, and the activities of consumers can extend these margins' (ibid.: 162). Interestingly, globalisation at once shares and super-sedes some of the brand's features. In fact, globalisation functions like a *meta-brand*, a brand of and about brand, for it is intangible and yet implies social relations, not only between different strata of society, but also between different ethnicities and economic and political groups. Globalisation is not fixed in time and space, but rather it defines a set of tendencies and relations between products and services and it is identifiable in its performance. It is at once hyper-real and the motor of world economy. Yet unlike other brands, globalisation does not distinguish between producers and con-sumers, for we are all, wherever we are, whoever we are, continuously partic-ipating in its performance.

There is something else that is characteristic of brand and constitutes a fundamental aspect of globalisation. Crucially, a brand

> is not and can never be completed. This is both the source of value of the brand as an object of contemporary capitalism (it is *a thing into which possibility has been introduced*), and what makes it open to other concerns.
>
> (ibid.: 163, added emphasis)

Globalisation too is open to possibility and is subject to negotiation. In other words, the economic movement designating the end of the sovereignty of the nation state, as well as the framework for our social life, is a complex and shifting meta-brand, marking the relations between the products and services we encounter in our daily lives. This meta-brand, at once affecting our economics, politics, culture and philosophy, is open to possibility. It is transformable. It is therefore not so much a matter of defining globalisation per se, since its shifting territory is subject to constant change, as analysing *whose* globalisation it is that we are actually performing in and *what* we need to do to ensure that this is a 'brand' that we actually wish to identify with.

Globalisation, or global culture, is associated with 'products, industries and technologies', which include, for instance, 'the growth of international tourism and the airline industries; multinational consumer brands such as Coca-Cola and Holiday Inns; popular media such as television soaps or disco music; or new electronic networks such as the Internet or satellite communication' (Franklin *et al.*, 2000: 2). In other words, global culture is not only a kind of brand, or meta-brand, but also a process, a medium and even a knowledge. Global is the brand name of what we wear, eat or drink. Global is also the process by which these commodities are produced and consumed. And finally, global is our interpretation, our reading of them as cultural products of a certain kind. Following this logic, everything we do is global and the global is everywhere. In other words, we exist in a global space and time and the global is our condition as well as our location, our actual *hic et nunc*.

Globalisation indicates and to some extent even legitimates a potential, though continuously modifiable, trajectory: from the local to the inter- and intra-national, from here to everywhere. However, as Zygmunt Bauman has shown, 'globalization divides as much as it unites' in that '[b]eing local in a globalized world is a sign of social deprivation and degradation' (1998: 2). This suggests that within the global world economy there are in fact two fundamental types of 'locality': the one that remains local, in that it is unable or unwilling to perform in the global communication network, and the one that is trans-local, inter-local, and even meta-local, in other words, global. So, globalisation shares with post-modernism not only its capacity to define an all-embracing condition, but also its ability to present itself as rhizomatic multiplicity, a continuously shifting and illusory paradigm. Both the product (or meta-brand) of capitalist discourse, they are able to cover global tendencies, manifest themselves rhizomatically and shift in their definition.

While globalisation identifies a utopia – the global, as a location for everybody – it also points out a paradox – the global breeds out of the local. And interestingly, globalisation exists not despite but because of this contradiction. As Bauman suggests, '[a]n integral part of the globalizing processes' is in fact formed by 'progressive spatial segregation, separation and exclusion'. Furthermore, still in Bauman's words, there is evidence of a 'progressive breakdown in communication between the increasingly global and extraterritorial elites and the ever more "localized" rest' (ibid.: 3). Therefore, the local always acts as both a constituent and a resistance to globalising processes and, while on the one hand, globalisation can be seen as a 'golden age of cosmopolitan "borderlessness"' (Urry, 2003: 6), on the other, in order to exist, it has not only to transcend the local but also to antagonise, or even annihilate it. In other words, the global not only creates, but also supports a divided geography.

Moreover, not only are there plural globalisations (Pieterse in Featherstone *et al.*, 1997: 45), but also the global is constituted by nothing but a plurality of locations. Thus, for instance, in his analysis of globalisation as 'glocalisation', Roland Robertson advocates that globalisation is not synonymous of homogenisation and that 'it makes no good sense to define the global as if the global excludes the local' (in Featherstone *et al.*, 1997: 34). Robertson instead asserts that globalisation 'has involved and increasingly involves the creation and the incorporation of locality, processes which themselves largely shape, in turn, the compression of the world as a whole' (ibid.: 40). Thus not only is globalisation an unstable phenomenon, seemingly aiming towards the incorporation of 'the peoples of the world [. . .] into a single world society, global society' (Albrow in Albrow and King, 1990: 45), but it is also constituted by an inherently Darwinian process through which various localities are in fact selected and propagated as 'global'. So globalisation indicates not so much a process of homologation, or even compression of the world, as one of performance, productivity, replication and simulation. In fact, globalisation is principally a means of (economic, political and cultural) production; it is the self-referential, cost-effective and predominantly simulated process by which capitalism propagates itself.

Globalisation is the 'open' meta-brand of capitalism. By being presented as globally available, a product or service implicitly becomes globally desirable, and thus globally sellable. And so the local becomes more effective as global. Rather than disempowering the local, this process elevates specific localities by branding them as global. But 'global' branding also has other implications. Michael Hardt and Antonio Negri in their now classic *Empire* (2000) argue that, following the collapse of Soviet barriers to the capitalist world market, there has been 'an irresistible and irreversible globalization of economic and cultural exchanges' which has led to a new form of sovereignty, namely empire, designating 'the political subject that effectively regulates these global exchanges, the sovereign power that governs the world' (ibid.: xi). Through the metaphor of empire, Hardt and Negri re-brand the cultural and political mechanisms at the heart of capitalist production processes. In their analysis, empire and globalisation are part of the same economy of discourse, but arguably, empire has more controversial implications because it presumes that an all-embracing and overshadowing agency is at the heart of it. Yet, as Hardt and Negri explain, empire is not identifiable with a nation state (ibid.) in that national and super-national organisms have merged in empire under a 'single logic of rule'. This rule has no territorial centre of power, nor does it rely on boundaries or barriers, but on the contrary it is a *'decentered* and *deterritorialising* apparatus' (ibid.: xii, original emphases). Moreover, here there are no first, second and third world divisions, but rather these are to be found within each other, in the sense that the first world can be found in the third, etc. (ibid.: xiii). In other words, there is no 'real' empire because, unlike at other historical points in time, there is no single nation state behind the power of empire. On the contrary, empire is both rhizomatic and utopic and, like globalisation, it is 'performed'.

The salient characteristic of empire is that it presents itself *above* history, thus fixing 'the existing state of affairs for eternity' (ibid.: xiv). Moreover, empire extends to all strata of the social system and aims to 'enlarge the realm of the consensus that supports its own power' (ibid.: 15). Empire also claims to resist a continuous crisis to international order (ibid.: 4) for which it has a 'right to intervention' (ibid.: 18); and although it 'is continually bathed in blood, the concept of Empire is always dedicated to peace' (ibid.: xiv). Finally, like post-modernism and globalisation, it indicates a condition and so its alternative is also contained within itself as a 'political organization of global flows and exchanges' (ibid.: xv). In other words, just as globalisation is 'open' to possibility, empire, the political subject that generates and regulates global exchanges, is still open enough to allow for change and potentially disclose the seeds of its own critique. What is needed therefore to highlight this critique is the identification of the mechanisms regulating empire itself. Thus Hardt and Negri, for instance, call for the identification of new critical languages (ibid.: 57) that are able to take into account that 'the virtual center of Empire can be attacked from any point' (ibid.: 59) and that 'the age of globalisation is the age of universal *contagion*' (ibid.: 136, added emphasis) precisely because it is the age which has disposed of outside and opposition so that everything is always already inside, always already part of empire and its globalising processes (ibid.: 187). This suggests that a critique of capitalist processes must and can only be produced by and within the processes that regulate it and that therefore it is *through* the actual modification of its performance, by means of *contamination of its branding*, that we are able to intervene in capitalist processes. In other words, radical artistic practices need to be utilising the very processes of empire, globalisation and capitalist production that they aim to critique.

Operating by playing with the semiotic ambiguity between economic, theatrical and discursive performance, radical practices can aesthetically subvert the mechanisms at the heart of globalisation and empire. Through the metaphor of empire Hardt and Negri highlight the very core of the connection between post-modernism, globalisation and capitalism. In doing so, they also set out how the terrain for contemporary political activism and militant art is not so much in opposition to post-modernism and globalisation, or even capitalism and empire, but rather 'hidden' within them. It is therefore not surprising that the main critique of these discourses and their economic manifestations has been taking place through *performance*, the art form that best identifies possibilities for the reading of liveness through discourse, and *media*, the main means by which contemporary society, whether economically, culturally, politically or artistically, is propagating itself.

One of the principal characteristics of post-modernity is the re-branding of society as an 'industry' of services. As Dave Renton points out, in this kind of society – for a society it still is – 'the world of production is becoming globalised, work becoming less important, and consumption more important' (2001: 5). This shift of focus from the producer to the consumer, from the social to the individual, from the nation state to the multinational corporation is a principal objective of both globalisation and empire. Giddens, for instance, observes that '[t]he sovereign consumer has replaced the ideas of the citizen and the public sphere' (2000: 12) and 'banking and insurance can be done over the Internet by companies bearing only a passing resemblance to those that have dominated these sectors; supermarkets sell domestic gas, while petrol stations double up as grocery stores and newsagents' (ibid.: 67). Thus globalisation has also implied the rewriting of identities and boundaries. While on the one hand it has advocated the multiplication of sameness, on the other it has generated cultural and economic difference in the ways we both produce and consume cultural, political and economic processes. This shift onto consumerism is also visible at the level of performance and the most effective practices within this sphere of performance activism tend to include some degree of interactivity, i.e. of consumer activity or even consumer empowerment, within them.

The world may increasingly be read as a 'global' economy, with even nature and the human body offering, through genetic manipulation and patenting, a space for productivity. This explains not only, as in Giddens's analysis, how the contemporary has become primarily a space of consumption, but also why the principal response to issues of globalisation and empire is also, by implication, through and about processes of consumption. And because by consumption one must not only understand the intake of 'real' goods, but also, perhaps even more importantly, the absorption of mediated ones, such as the consumption of information by and through the media, it becomes clear why in our society of spectacle any political discourse that wishes to engage with globalisation or empire must first and foremost engage with media control. Both empire and globalisation are meta-brands whose scope and even legitimacy are created through the production and distribution of certain qualities of information. Neither meta-brand exists outside of the information generating them. To control the information at the heart of them means to control what they are. In this post-modern society, it is those who own, produce and control information that are able to rule 'globally', economically as well as politically. Unsurprisingly, the battle over information is already at the heart of the wars that are being fought around us, so arguably the fight for the control over information increasingly amounts to a fight for the control of our actual lives.

Resistance: theatre as hacktivism

The neologism hacktivism designates a form of activism that manifests itself through electronic civic disobedience and similar Internet-related activities. Like other forms of activism, hacktivism is politically driven but, unlike them, it is not necessarily identifiable with a permanent objective or a specific political movement. In hacktivism the activity is in fact often rhizomatic, contagious and metamorphic. Through the Internet, hacktivists are able to reach 'global' audiences in what can be described as resistant, global and performative forms of practice. Like other types of political resistance, hacktivism conducts limited but effective actions aiming to raise awareness through disruption. Hacktivist strategies may therefore include distributing information through the web, alerting viewers and sporadically even diverting them from their navigation, offering software and cloning websites. Occasionally dissent has been expressed by overwhelming specific servers or websites via email barricades created by thousands of protest messages. In other instances, computer viruses and worms were created to 'penetrate' specific sites and addresses. Although hacktivism shares some characteristics with hacking in terms of technique, it otherwise distances itself from it. Both hacking and hacktivism are 'about knowledge, and hence about power' (Riemens in Stocker and Schöpf, 1998: 47), but hacktivism is more directly politically driven and thus ultimately artistically and socially oriented. Moreover, hacktivism offers no personal gain. Quite the contrary, it aims to alert viewers to what are perceived to constitute political and social injustices. As suggested by its principal theorists, Critical Art Ensemble, 'hacking is done primarily as a form of digital resistance rather than as an idiosyncratic activity or as a profit, or prestige generating process' (in Meikle, 2002: 141). By utilising the web as a form of protest, hacktivism often attempts to 'globalise' local concerns, or rather glocalise them, thereby drawing attention to the fact that local issues can often and indeed should be of global consequence.

Although there are substantial distinctions between hackers and hacktivists, the latter often utilise imagery and techniques employed by the former. Hackers, for instance, work secretly to protect their identity. Hacktivists also tend to present themselves anonymously, often utilising their company's name as their *brand*. But whereas hackers work in disguise, hacktivists tend to act *in character*. In other words, whereas in hacking the deception is often invisible, in hacktivism the main action consists of the propagation of an idea through a performative process. And, whereas hacking is all about trespass and violation, often lacking direction and overall vision, hacktivism constitutes the first organised attempt to use the Internet for radical artistic and political purposes. So whereas hacking may ultimately challenge the law in the name of individualism and freedom, hacktivism tends to stay within the law, for its aim is not so much to trespass as to share information. In fact on the rare occasions when hacktivism has been outside the law, it has tended to precipitate a crisis to produce a change in the law or, at least, to draw the public's attention to what is perceived to be a social or political injustice. In other words, hacktivism's perhaps most significant and original feature has been its ability to work from within the world of information. More than any other artistic or political movement, hacktivism is showing us that we need to pay attention to the fact that the battle for the control of information is not simply a question of aesthetics but of social and political survival. In fact what is ultimately at stake in the work of the various hacktivist communities that are currently active is the control over the production, manipulation and distribution of information. What they remind us of, is that information equals knowledge and *knowledge equals real, concrete power.*

Hacktivists often act by means of simulation and digital invasion: 'theirs is an engaged politics that seeks solutions in software' (ibid.: 141). Through simulation, they draw attention to the fact that on the Internet notions of authorship, individualism, privacy and even freedom of speech need to be (re-)defined. Through digital invasion, they show how easy it is to adopt and penetrate digital identities belonging to other individuals or organisations. This is because on the Internet our identities are of course signalled through information. So on the world wide web, it is not so much the control of productivity but the control of knowledge, of information, that determines who is in charge. Hacktivists claim that this tendency towards the private ownership of information already defines other areas of productivity in society. Thus, McKenzie Wark, the author of *A Hacker Manifesto*, shows, increasingly how we witness leading corporations

> divest themselves of their productive capacity, as this is no longer a source of power. They rely on a competing mass of capitalist contractors for the manufacture of their products. Their power lies in monopolizing intellectual property – patents, copyrights and trademarks – and the means of reproducing their value – the vectors of communication. *The privatisation of information becomes the dominant, rather than a subsidiary, aspect of commodified life.*
>
> (2004: 032, emphasis added)

Hacktivist protest is about digital citizenship. In this age of control, theirs is increasingly turning into a battle for the wider distribution of the means of control over information.

One of the principal ways in which hacktivists and other net artists have been able to draw attention to the politics of information, is by alerting computer users to the fact that online they are at the same time more powerful but also more vulnerable than in real life. By experimenting with the viewer's perception and interaction with the computer interface, a number of practices have shown, for instance, how the computer is not only a means by which the viewer can connect with and on occasion even participate in wider artistic, social or political events but also a gateway through which they could become exposed to and even contaminated by external agents. The computer interface, often used prosthetically, as a portal through which to enter the world wide web – the location where the private becomes public – is therefore both a means of empowering the viewer as well as a site of exposure. Not only do we become susceptible to viruses and worms, or whatever creatures are sent our way, but we also increasingly need to defend ourselves from a mounting quantity of unwanted information, and so the control over information also implies the control over the tools that protect us from an excess of information (unwanted advertising, pornography, Internet poker, scam emails and the like). Our computer interface is not only indicative of who we are and how we organise ourselves, but also of what we work with, need in our daily lives and feel rewarded by, personally or socially, aesthetically and politically. In other words, the interface is our dress, our façade to the world. From the way we *appear* online, an enormous amount of information about ourselves is derived, utilised and ultimately commercially exploited.

The company which has most successfully and disturbingly problematised the interface, at least from an aesthetic point of view, are the Dutch–Belgian artists Joan Heemskerk and Dirk Paesmans who since 1995 have operated under the name JODI. Working primarily by manipulating HTML code so that the viewer is no longer able to distinguish between code and art, JODI create complex metatextual and intermedial artworks that often, like *OSS/***** (1998), create the impression of an irretrievable computer error.

> If you click the mouse hoping to get rid of this computer virus or whatever it is, windows open up everywhere, your cursor starts leaving a trail, your pull-down menus become either empty or unintelligible, thick horizontal stripes start running across your screen, suddenly changing into vertical ones. There is no escape. And in the unlikely event that you do escape, your pointer becomes invisible and you must click on one of the many plus signs of the screen in order to get away.
>
> (Mulder and Post, 2000: 99)

Not only do JODI physicalise the viewer's experience of the computer (ibid.: 100), but they also visualise how difficult it is to distinguish between a 'real error' and one that is designed to occur for aesthetic purposes. By simulating the collapse of the interface, and thereby alluding to the catastrophe of the world of information at the heart of it, JODI transform this seemingly neutral space into a theatre, thereby drawing attention not only to its public quality but also to the fact that the interface is the site where the digital battle over the control of information we store in our computers, i.e. the battle over the control of our digital selves, takes place. But with JODI, despite the persuasiveness of the collapse of the interface, the viewer is still fairly safe.

When in September 1999 a clone of JODI's website appeared on the web, which was not clearly distinguishable from the original and was in fact mistaken by many for the original, it also became apparent that not only was the world wide web a space of control but also, potentially, of deception. This site was generated by the Italian group 0100101110101101.ORG who wanted to demonstrate that 'certain ideas and practices – such as the authenticity and uniqueness of an artwork – must be considered obstacles to the development of web art' (0100101110101101.ORG, 2002). By operating anonymously as hacktivists, 0100101110101101.ORG aim to destabilise the web as a 'safe' environment and expose how issues of control, simulation and cloning are really at the heart of the society of information. For 0100101110101101.ORG, performing the web means exposing the vulnerability of the viewer in their capacity to deal with (interpret, trust, own) online information (see Figure 2.1).

In this context 0100101110101101.ORG developed a number of clone sites, such as *vaticano.org* (1998) in which they created and maintained for an entire year a clone of the official Vatican site (ibid.); *hell.com* (1999) in which a copy was made of the leading net art museum (ibid.); and *Ftpermutations* (2001) where the directory naming 12 artists participating in the Korea Web Art Festival was substituted with another site (ibid.). 0100101110101101.ORG also created web art viruses such as in *biennale.py* (2001) where, in response to an invitation to participate in the 49th Biennale in Venice, the company created a bug which was spread from the Slovene Pavilion on the opening day of the exhibition (ibid.). From these

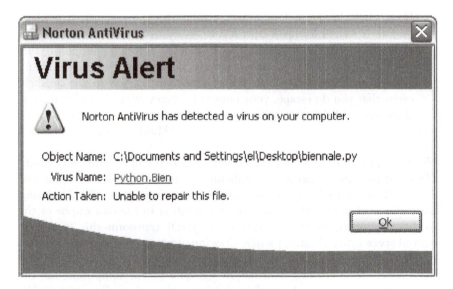

Figure 2.1 04 biennale.py – alert.gif. 0100101110101101.ORG (Eva and Franco Mattes). Biennale.py Norton Antivirus Alert. 2001. Screenshot (source: Courtesy of 0100101110101101.ORG).

examples, it is clear that 0100101110101101.ORG ultimately aim to expose the vulnerability of privacy and copyright on the web. In *Vopos* (2002), for instance, they allowed for the constant virtual monitoring of the location of two members of the group via telephone, satellite and the Internet (ibid.) and in the earlier piece *life_sharing* (2001), they shared their files on the web, thus drawing attention to the fact that the information we store on our machines is always already much more public than we think. Not only is the problematic of control absolutely crucial to our digital existence but it is also a determining factor in our society's ability to own the knowledge it produces. What motivates hacktivism is ultimately a defence of citizenship and ownership of knowledge and the belief that only by maintaining control over the world of information, will our systems of democracy survive as we know them.

Electronic Disturbance Theater

The Electronic Disturbance Theater (EDT) is constituted by a group of net artists and activists whose principal aim has been the disturbance, through electronic actions, of Mexican government sites. This has been to draw attention to the conflict that since the mid 1990s has devastated the lives of the people from the Mexican region of Chiapas. In fact the company's first action was in response to the massacre of 45 indigenous civilians, including children, at the hands of paramilitary groups in December 1997. Founded by the performer and former member of Critical Art Ensemble, Ricardo Dominguez, in collaboration with Stefan Wray, Carmin Karasic, and Brett Stalbaum in early 1998, EDT claims to have been influenced by Bertold Brecht, Augusto Boal, and Teatro Campesino (Dominguez in Lane, 2003: 132) and describes its work as a 'hybrid between Augusto Boal's Invisible Theatre and a Situationist gesture' (Dominguez in Fusco, 2003: 156). EDT's activities are also unquestionably inspired by the Zapatista movement's own 'theatrical' and 'informational' warfare tactics. As suggested by Manuel Castells, the Zapatistas were the '*first informational guerrilla movement*. They created a media event in order to diffuse their message, while desperately trying not to be brought into a bloody war' (1997: 79, original emphasis). This tactic, so widely employed by activists worldwide, was also at the heart of EDT's work. Just as 'the Zapatista's own recombinant theatre of operations meshed virtual and embodied practices in a struggle for real material change and social well-being in Chiapas' (Lane, 2003: 135), EDT's own theatre also aimed to penetrate the real through the virtual, to raise awareness and thus potentially effect social change (see Figure 2.2).

EDT's theatre is constituted by INFOacts, theatrical protest actions expressed through and about information. On 18 January 1998 Dominguez called for a NetStrike for Zapata. This call asked for solidarity with the Zapatista movement by means of the blockage of a series of Internet sites. The blockage was to be achieved by pressing the reload button several times over

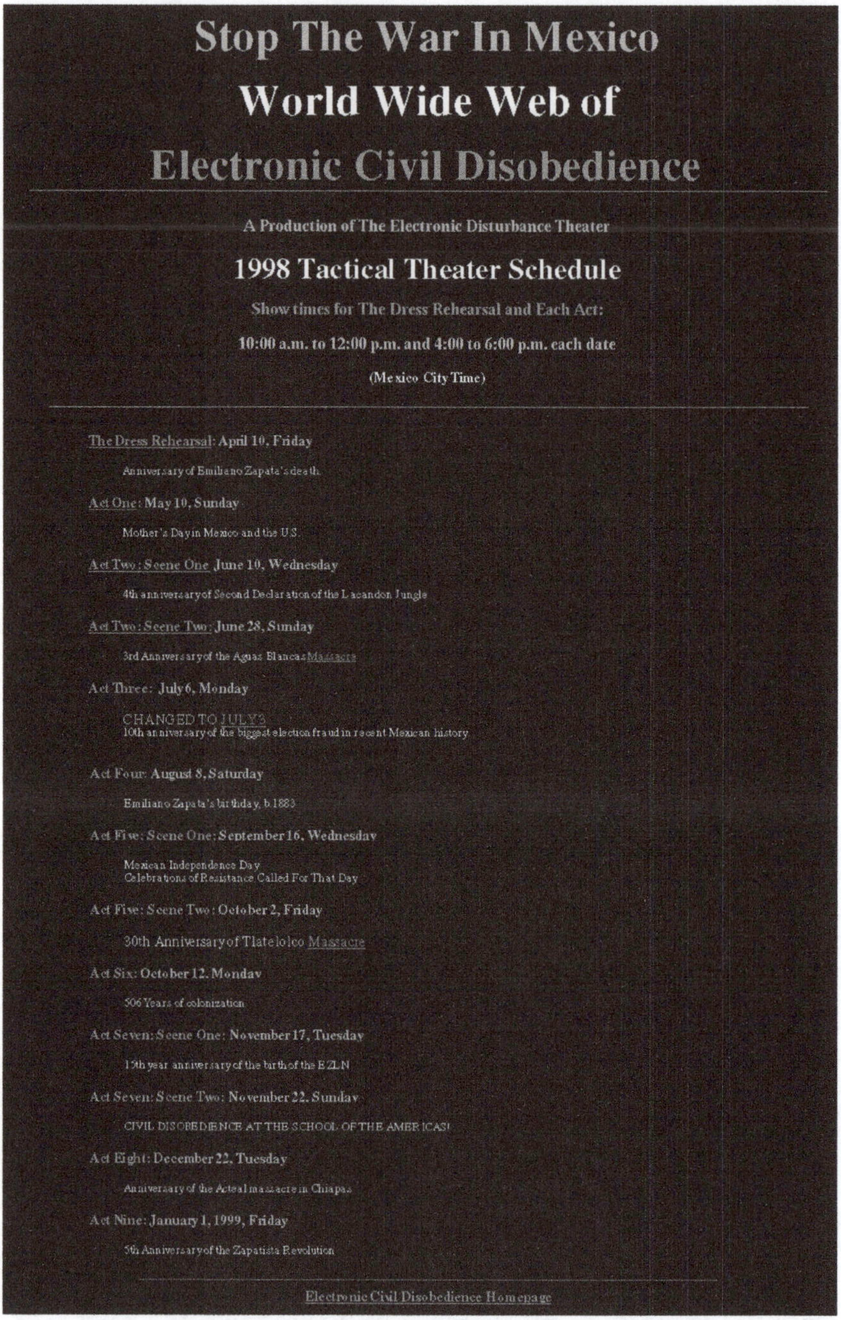

Stop The War In Mexico
World Wide Web of
Electronic Civil Disobedience

A Production of The Electronic Disturbance Theater

1998 Tactical Theater Schedule

Show times for The Dress Rehearsal and Each Act:

10:00 a.m. to 12:00 p.m. and 4:00 to 6:00 p.m. each date

(Mexico City Time)

The Dress Rehearsal: April 10, Friday

Anniversary of Emiliano Zapata's death.

Act One: May 10, Sunday

Mother's Day in Mexico and the U.S.

Act Two: Scene One June 10, Wednesday

4th anniversary of Second Declaration of the Lacandon Jungle

Act Two: Scene Two: June 28, Sunday

3rd Anniversary of the Aguas Blancas Massacre

Act Three: July 6, Monday

CHANGED TO JULY 5
10th anniversary of the biggest election fraud in recent Mexican history

Act Four: August 8, Saturday

Emiliano Zapata's birthday, b.1883

Act Five: Scene One: September 16, Wednesday

Mexican Independence Day
Celebrations of Resistance Called For That Day

Act Five: Scene Two: October 2, Friday

30th Anniversary of Tlatelolco Massacre

Act Six: October 12, Monday

506 Years of colonization

Act Seven: Scene One: November 17, Tuesday

15th year anniversary of the birth of the EZLN

Act Seven: Scene Two: November 22, Sunday

CIVIL DISOBEDIENCE AT THE SCHOOL OF THE AMERICAS!

Act Eight: December 22, Tuesday

Anniversary of the Acteal massacre in Chiapas

Act Nine: January 1, 1999, Friday

5th Anniversary of the Zapatista Revolution

Electronic Civil Disobedience Homepage

Figure 2.2 Extract from EDT's home page (since 1998) (source: Courtesy of Ricardo Dominguez, Carmin Karasic, Brett Stalbaum, and Stefan Wray).

a period of an hour. The actions took place over the period of a year. EDT achieved this through FloodNet, a software tool able to 'autonomate requests to a target webpage, and in doing so, disturb a website' (ibid.: 139). By repeatedly accessing the webpage, for instance, of the Mexican President Ernesto Zedillo, and requesting non-existent files containing phrases like 'human rights' and 'justice', error messages were caused that then circulated around the world.

> For the duration of the flood-performance, the automatic reload requests compelled the targeted sites to produce – to *perform* – a kind of electronic social revelation. In just one iteration, the FloodNet repeatedly requested non-existent pages, with such names as 'justice' or 'human rights' from the Mexican government site, compelling the server to produce a steady, flashing stream of '404 error-reply' messages stating: 'justice not found on this site' and 'human rights not found on this site'.
>
> (ibid., added emphasis)

The programme also left on the machine the names of the people who had been killed in the repression. The aim was to send a clear message to the global economy that protest, even local protest, had the capacity of going global. 'EDT has placed the very notion of "embodiment" under rigorous question, and sought to understand the specific possibilities for constructing *presence* in digital space that is both *collective* and *politicised*' (ibid.: 131, original emphases). Through FloodNet, individuals from different parts of the world were able to reconstitute themselves as a political community. And thus the virtual became able to reclaim the real, *en masse.*

On 9 September 1998 EDT staged a FloodNet performance at the Ars Electronica Festival in Linz, Austria. The protest, which lasted 24 hours and involved over 10,000 people, was directed against President Zedillo's home page, but also at the Frankfurt Stock Exchange and the Pentagon websites. The operation received multiple hostile responses.

> At 7.30 that morning, says Dominguez, I received a phone call from an individual with a very clear Mexican Spanish accent, who I can only say must have been a Mexican agent. They said: 'Is this Ricardo Domiguez?' 'Yes.' 'Of the Electronic Disturbance Theater?' 'Yes.' They said in very clear Spanish: 'We know where you are at, we know what you are going to do, we know where your family lives. Do not go downstairs, do not start this performance, you know that this is not a game.'
>
> (Dominguez in Meikle, 2002: 151)

As a consequence of this threat, Dominguez reports, he not only went ahead with the 'performance' but also contacted the press. 'Part of this performance', he comments, 'is to create this *drama*, creating a situation where the politics of the space play without me having to go "Oh, look at the mean bad people." People actually *see* the mean bad people doing their mean bad thing' (ibid., added emphases).

However, telephone threats were not the only response to this project. While the Mexican Spanish voice was utilising conventional means to frighten off the company, the US services launched an informatic counterattack. So a Java applet, similar to EDT's own, was used as a countermeasure, and the computers of those who had participated in the digital sit-in were contaminated through it. This of course raised the issue of what kind of response might be appropriate to an act of digital disturbance (ibid.: 154–5) and whether an overall blind attack on all who had participated was not equivalent to 'shooting into the crowd'. Since ultimately no 'real' damage had been done, why were the secret services, or whoever actually launched the applet, even interested in responding to this provocation? Why was this INFOact turned into an INFOwar? 'FloodNet never accessed or destroyed any data, nor tampered with security, nor changed websites, nor crashed servers' (Karasic in ibid.: 164), so what were the reasons for this particular response? As Philip Schlesinger suggests, '[r]eal political outcomes are at stake [. . .] if the public can be persuaded that the state is right, this helps mobilise support for transferring resources from welfare to security. Language matters, and how the media use language matters' (in ibid.: 160). Although in many ways EDT's operation was simply an act of theatrical protest, with the Internet used as a stage, the means utilised were so ingenious and effective that a disproportionate response was deemed necessary, simply to prevent anyone from using the world wide web in this way again. This of course did not deter EDT, which on 1 January 1999 released a *Disturbance Developers Kit*, including FloodNet, which in many ways led to the beginning of international hacktivism (ibid.).

EDT's work is complex and hybrid in nature. Performing at the intersection of 'radical politics, recombinant activism, performance art, and software design' (Dominguez in Lane, 2003: 132), EDT has been exploiting performance's ability to represent and interfere with life. Structurally, their references are explicitly artistic, even theatrical.

> Each performance has a very traditional three-act structure: act 1, the e-mail call to a core actor/audience network (you may also start to get responses from reporters for information and updates); act 2, the gesture itself, which is not very interesting to look at since you don't really see that much – you just click (click = action); act three, you re-encounter your core actor/audience network to determine what might have occurred within your staging space, how many people participated, where they came from, what they might have said, and of course what has been reported about the performance.
>
> (Dominguez in Fusco, 2003: 151)

Interestingly though, the hybridity is not only perceivable at this level but also in terms of the 'collapse [in] the space of difference between the real body and the electronic body, between everyday life and everyday life online, between the activist and the hacker, the performer and the audience, individual agency and mass-swarming' (Dominguez in ibid.: 152). Thus at the heart of their work is not only a contamination of modes and means of information but also of audiences and actors:

> the actions force a rethinking of their own networked subjectivity as 'hackers', 'activists', 'actors', and 'audiences'. EDT's staging compel[s] these actor/audience networks to encounter each other. In other words, members of each group face a challenge to their identity: hackers used to secrecy have to 'come out', activists committed to working in the street meet online, and actors and audiences accustomed to purely fictional representations of reality with no social repercussions to their engagement find themselves in a simulation that does have a visible impact on the social.
>
> (ibid.)

And so, a theatrical act, with a theatrical structure, is enacted by its spectators, who become its actors, through the Internet, i.e. virtually, but towards a real effect. As noted by Coco Fusco in an interview with Dominguez, in their work the Internet definitely constitutes 'a *dramatic scenario that can facilitate social and political engagement with issues in the off-line world*' (2003: 151, emphasis added).

Electronic Civil Disobedience, EDT's principal means of protest, is a term created by Critical Art Ensemble and then developed by Anonymous Digital Coalition, an Italian political hacktivist group, for the first digital sit-in on 12 December 1995 in opposition to the French government's nuclear policies (Meikle, 2002: 150). Through the actions of EDT, Electronic Civil Disobedience became known as a powerful and efficient means of civil protest. Over 18,000 participants, for instance, were drawn in, in just over two hours, from locations as far apart as South Africa, Hong Kong and Iceland for EDT's INFOact against the Mexican government (ibid.: 144). One of the legacies of EDT's work is to have shown us that the Internet, through its ability not only to reach distant communities but also to create *communitas* among them, can be a formidable and 'global' tool for spreading information and creating political presence. EDT has also demonstrated how vulnerable a world it still is, for although the off-line citizen is protected by the law when undue violence is utilised in a protest, the digital citizen is currently exposed to informatic annihilation. EDT's work, like most forms of hacktivism, is undoubtedly artistically and politically provocative, but it is so peacefully, in the spirit of a long tradition of socially and politically oriented theatre. And as in the words of Dominguez, it is important to remember that 'all of this electronic activism is about a real community in search of real peace' (in Stocker and Schöpf, 1998: 55).

etoy

The company etoy has been active online since 1994. On its website, which embraces the aesthetic, principally in terms of jargon and layout, of a corporation website, it presents itself as a 'controversial global player' with a corporate structure, or 'sculpture', able 'to maximise cultural value' (etoy, 2004). The success of this aesthetic is such that when I first asked a group of students to investigate the company, they could not work out what they were looking for and came back to the class reporting that, although they thought that they had understood the company's objectives, they felt that they had failed to identify a product and an overall mission. Etoy, they argued, utilises the aesthetic, structure and branding, but not the 'usual' content, of a global business corporation website. In fact etoy *is* a corporation. However, as my students had not failed to notice, on the etoy website there is actually no 'conventional' product to be sold. In fact, etoy does not 'sell isolated art objects' but rather it 'sells, trades and exchanges parts of itself' (ibid.). In other words, etoy offers to sell 'nothing' but its own brand and it is precisely the act, or play, of performing, producing and selling this brand that is at the heart of their work.

The website aesthetic is of course quite deliberately misleading. The mission, etoy claims, is to address 'the dramatic problems of globalisation', something which it believes cannot 'be solved by simply rejecting global markets, economic exchange that drive companies, culture, individuals and politics' but by adopting and exploiting the very mechanisms that it critiques. The company's objective, or etoy.operations, is thus constituted by the exploration and indeed exploitation of its own 'social, cultural and financial value'. Thus etoy.CORPORATION 'crosses and blurs the frontiers between art, identity, nations, fashion, politics, technology, social engineering, music, power and business to create massive impacts on global markets and digital culture' (ibid.). While on the one hand etoy makes its own commercial inaction, its resistance to capitalistic processes, its own value, it also attempts to 'sell' this value globally to maximise public awareness about itself as an alternative type of subversive art-making corporation.

But exactly what kind of corporation is etoy? In the past etoy's core corporate image was quite militaristic. Male performers, shaven-haired, wearing mirrored dark sunglasses, striking orange uniforms and behaving in a regimented manner, behaved as if on a life-threatening mission. Although this image has not altered substantially throughout the years, it has grown in complexity. Thus the core of the company is now formed by four women and 11 men, physically located between Austria, Switzerland, Italy, Germany, Japan and the USA. The web, they now claim, 'is the place of our existence, the body is not important' (ibid.). The company is in fact owned by its own shareholders (on occasion totalling almost 2,000 participants) who 'invest time, knowledge, and ideas (or simply finance)' into the enterprise. Thus etoy.SHAREHOLDERS are meant to 'participate in dynamic artwork that takes place 24 hours a day in the middle of society – on and offline' (ibid.). Although the directive of the company itself is still constituted by the core of the group, it is the less visible but, on occasion, very active multitude behind and beyond the centre, whether as etoy.SHAREHOLDERS or etoy.AGENTS, that renders their work aesthetically complex, and politically and economically effective (see Figure 2.3).

In the past, activities have physically taken place in San Diego, San Francisco, New York, Madrid, Turin, Amsterdam, Tokyo and Ljubliana (ibid.). These sites are represented online as branches of etoy's central offices in Zürich. Again, the images from these different locations do not so much suggest regional variation as reflect global branding. Wherever they are, etoy agents are identical to themselves, for they do not constitute so much a group of people as a brand. As Rachel Greene suggests, theirs is an 'office aesthetics' (2004: 65), with everything, from uniform costumes, to looks, and even transportation, mocking the anonymity and potential loss of subjectivity imposed by its own corporate branding. Claiming that their corporate identity is their entire content, etoy.AGENTS, constituted by individuals willing to participate in etoy actions, are said to be functioning as 'interchangeable elements of a digital program'. Since 1998 the company has also been using orange etoy.TANKS, '12 and 6 meter long standardized windowless shipping containers – the icons of globalisation' as a 'mobile and multifunctional office system including studios, hotels, conference rooms etc' so that 'wherever etoy is needed in the physical world, the orange etoy tanks pop up or vanish over night to infect the way people think and feel' (etoy, 2004). These offices, orange boxes with no windows, fitted out with cables for light and electricity and digital data processing as well as internal and external communication, are the recognisable non-space from which etoy's actions are launched: not so much a 'real' space as a portal from which to gain access to information.

The company, which won the prestigious Golden Nica (1996) for *digital hijack* and regularly appears on television and in various media, both 'invited and uninvited', 'to inject etoy.VIRUS' where needed (etoy, 2004), is best known for *digital hijack* (1996) and *toywar* (1999–2000). Both pieces are engaged with information control and advanced our knowledge of what was possible on and through the Internet. *Digital hijack*, quite literally, consisted of the virtual hijack of 'anyone who typed words such as "Madonna" or "Playboy" into search machines like Yahoo or Altavista' (ibid.). In fact the list of words that triggered the hijack was quite long, and so the chance of being hijacked, especially if engaging with music, art, film, but also politics, for instance, was probably relatively high. During *digital hijack* hundreds of thousands of unaware online surfers became quite literally trapped in a website by the name hijack.org, which said: 'You have been digitally hijacked by the organization etoy. Don't fucking move' (in Baumgärtel,

Figure 2.3 Six etoy.CORE-AGENTS, the crew that established the etoy. NIPPON-BRANCH in Tokyo enter the Asia market (source: Copyright, 2001: hiroshi masuyama).

2001: 218–19). Through this provocative piece, etoy demonstrated how easy it is to control online information and not only dictate what viewers see but also, quite literally, affect their ability to move and thereby restrict their freedom and right to information. The digital citizen, etoy shows here, is always already hijacked by the systems used to navigate online.

Toywar on the other hand, arose out of necessity. Unexpectedly, etoy found itself sued by the US-based dotcom toy business eToys for alleged infringement of its trademark rights even though the company's Internet address was actually registered three years before the American corporation registered its own site. EToys, concerned that clients would mistake etoy for them, first offered to buy the etoy site and then demanded that it close its site or pay $10,000 each day the site was kept open. Etoy immediately moved into exile on another site but in doing so alerted a number of lists. The international support was such that etoy turned it into a global campaign. Over 2,000 etoy.AGENTS were recruited and encouraged to express their support, in whatever way they felt appropriate, including disruption. For each act of sabotage, points were scored. This was the beginning of *TOYWAR*, a multi-user action entertainment game, that created the sense of a huge battlefield in which users could fight against eToys, enjoy their own character and income, etoy.SHARE options and even the power to make decisions affecting the company's future.

> That *Toywar*, despite its very real legal stakes and the substantial monies involved, was called a 'game' by its producers suggests a new dimension to art practices brought on by internet technologies. Using the premise of fighting against an enemy and defending space, as well as the *FloodNet* applet, and an element of performance, tactical media asserted itself as a method for seizing or reclaiming public space.
>
> (Greene, 2004: 127)

And the more powerful etoy became, the more money eToys offered to either shut the site down or to take it over, alongside its trademark, so that the total amount of money presented by eToys to etoy went from $160,000 to $520,000 (see Figure 2.4).

During the period preceding the trial, etoy had effectively launched what has been described as an 'infowar' (Baumgärtel, 2001: 218). The action was supported by ®TMark, THE THING, EDT, Rhizome.org and other powerful lists. In fact, ®TMark designed the infowar campaign, which it called *The Twelve Days of Christmas*, while EDT allowed for the use of its *FloodNet*, and emails and other postings were employed to effectively 'interrupt the toy seller's website and reputation during the busiest sales period of the year' (Greene, 2004: 126). As a consequence of the campaign, eToys' stock price fell by more than 40 per cent (ibid.: 127), the lawsuit was resolved, the company declared bankrupt and etoy reimbursed by eToys for up to $40,000 in legal fees. Etoy celebrated through the following email:

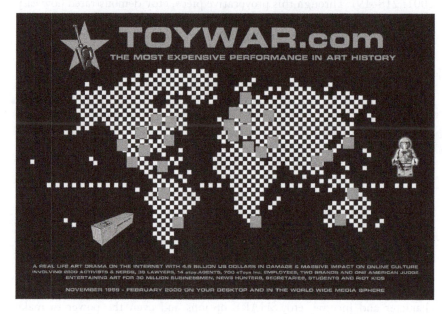

Figure 2.4 TOYWAR.map 2000, showing some of the locations in the real world from which TOYWAR.agents coordinated their counterstrike against eToys INC's multi-billion-dollar empire (source: Copyright 2000: the TOYWAR.community represented by the etoy.VC group).

TOTAL VICTORY for the etoy.CORPORATION AND THE INTERNET COMMUNITY (WHICH PROVED THAT THE NET IS NOT YET IN THE HANDS OF E-COMMERCE GIANTS).

(etoy, 2004)

The virtual war designed like a computer game, and provoked by a battle over the control of a digital domain name, had had a real casualty (Figure 2.5).

The remarkable conclusion to this digital conflict was that etoy, a group of 'media artists who work with information viruses' (Baumgärtel, 2001: 221), was actually able to defeat a 'real' dotcom business. Described as the first to 'use dotcom aesthetics to reposition art in relation to daily practices' (Greene, 2004: 65), etoy demonstrated that an artistic, digital campaign could have real, longlasting, political and economic consequences. It is clear from this piece that because '[t]he borders between real companies and such "art companies" are completely obscured' (etoy in Baumgärtel, 2001: 222), art companies could effectively enter the global market and 'perform' in their own right. By deliberately creating an aesthetic in which the boundaries between art, life *and* economics are blurred, etoy allows for a contamination of genres that enables it to be active at all these levels.

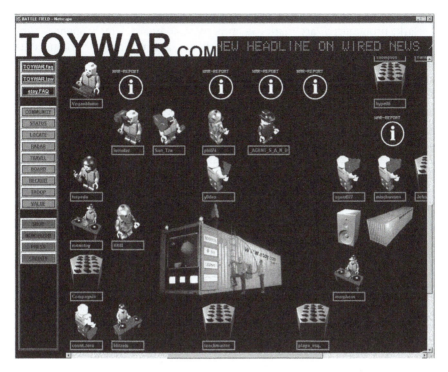

Figure 2.5 TOYWAR.battlefield on the Internet: showing some of the 2,500
TOYWAR.agents in January 2000, two weeks before eToys INC. signed
a settlement and dropped its lawsuit against etoy (source: Copyright
2000: the TOYWAR.soldiers represented by the etoy.VC group).

> We don't want to be coded. We're not Net activists, we're not hackers,
> and we're not skinheads. You can't peg us; that's our main quality. It's
> not really clear what we are. [. . .] Art has to have an impact on society.
> Art has to confront the most important issues of its time. We deal with
> shares, with the stock market and with big corporations because it's the
> most relevant theme of our time.

> (ibid.: 229)

Etoy had to protect its brand name because that was all that it had. In this
sense, etoy is pure signifier. Through *toywar* etoy was able to use art as 'an
incubator that turns the essence of digital lifestyle, e-commerce and society
into cultural value' (etoy in Greene, 2004: 65). Whereas EDT's more explicitly political actions had ultimately only succeeded in raising public awareness, *toywar* had an actual economic effect. As pointed out by Dominguez,
'perhaps as we become more virtual in the future, electronic civil disobedience may become a more useful tool. Not just as a symbolic efficacy, but
as a means for really leveraging activist concerns' (in Meikle, 2002: 170).

®TMark and The Yes Men

®TMark, pronounced 'art mark', is an activist company which finances subversive activities and interventions, both on- and offline. ®TMark uses its mailing lists to raise support for a variety of causes. Its site lists projects that are funded as well as those that still require funding. Typically, anything from $1,000 to $5,000 suffices for a large project. The company claim that an investment in ®TMark is an investment in culture and visitors are encouraged to spend with them on the promise of 'cultural dividends' (in Meikle, 2002: 116). So, by sending funds to ®TMark, one becomes 'an investor in ®TMark' (®TMark, 2005).

®TMark's primary field of action is within the interface of the spheres of economics and performance – an artistic performance aimed towards the aesthetic contamination of political and economic performance processes. Thus the company supports

> the sabotage – or as they might put it, the informative alteration – of corporate products, from dolls and children's learning tools to electronic action games, by channelling funds from investors into 'mutual funds', set up to pay for the production of specific art projects by 'workers'. [. . .] while regular corporations function to increase wealth for shareholders, sometimes regardless of cultural or social implications, ®TMark works towards improving its constituents' lives, sometimes at the expense of corporate practices.
>
> (Greene, 2004: 94)

Members of the company often present themselves using fake names and alternate identities, partly to mock the protection offered to business corporations. Formed by two artists working under the assumed names of Ray Thomas and Frank Guerrero, later joined by Candid Lucida, who respectively claim to be a schoolteacher, a lawyer and a financial analyst living in Los Angeles, San Francisco and New York, ®TMark 'don't just criticise corporation – they *are* a corporation. And they don't just sneer at corporate language, they appropriate it, all the better to subvert it' (Meikle, 2002: 126) (see Figure 2.6).

®TMark operates both digitally and performatively. In fact, members often perform through digital contaminations. Thus, for instance, they facilitated the cloning of websites for a number of politicians and companies, such as *gwbush.com*, a fake website for George W. Bush in which they exposed his former 'alleged cocaine abuse' (Baumgärtel, 2001: 107) and to which Bush's response, in front of a number of television cameras, appears to be: 'there ought to be limits to freedom!' (in Meikle, 2002: 113). Naturally, the prank registered a considerable media interest and the fake Bush site received almost six million hits whereas Bush's official site managed only 30,000 hits in the same period (ibid.: 117). ®TMark also publicised a separate group's

Figure 2.6 Yes Man Snafu demonstrates the Bush cowboy suit, whose gas-nozzle sidearms fire streams of oil-coloured confetti. The suit did not dissuade Bush supporters from asking him for campaign bumper stickers (source: Courtesy of The Yes Men).

protest against Jörg Haider and his Austrian Freedom Party. In this case 'the media brouhaha that follows [constituted] an important part of the overall action' (Baumgärtel, 2001: 107), demonstrating once again that an important part of hacktivist 'performance' consists of media exposure and that, to a certain degree, 'activism means being publicly exposed in the media' (ibid.: 109).

®TMark, which also famously switched Barbie and G.I. Joe dolls' voice boxes (1993) and interfered with a Sims computer game (1997) by inserting homoerotic images of two boys kissing, is an online centre, managing and publicising funding for the artistic sabotage of what are perceived to be economic and political targets. Their aim is to organise and provide funding 'for subversive activities and the sabotage of products' and then to 'publicize these actions so they get a lot of media attention.' To do this, ®TMark exploits a legal paradox:

> We operate in the same way a corporation does. In the US, corporations have the same legal rights as individuals. That's how people who run corporations deflect their risks. If the company kills somebody or wipes out a village in Mexico, they are not personally liable, but rather their corporation assumes this liability. [. . .] The American artists collective Act Up was one of the early models for this. They realised that activism in the late 20th century means being publicly exposed in the media because otherwise no one takes any notice of you at all. If you just do a subversive action and no one knows about it, it hasn't really happened.
>
> (in Baumgärtel, 2001: 107)

According to Graham Meikle, ®TMark's aim is to 'draw attention to the system of corporate power, rather than to the activities of any particular corporation' (2002: 114). The company achieves this by exploiting the fact that American corporations have enjoyed the same rights as individual citizens since the *Santa Clara County v. Southern Pacific Railroad* case of 1886 in which the Supreme Court ruled that corporations were protected under the 14th Amendment, which in fact had been written to protect the rights of free slaves. Because ®TMark is itself a registered corporation that enables 'non-life threatening', 'commercial sabotage', it is paradoxically protected by the very law it aims to expose.

The company's best-known intervention so far was at the expense of the World Trade Organisation (WTO). On 20 November 1999 the WTO found that a competing website had been set up at www.gatt.org (World Trade Organisation/GATT Home Page) questioning the value of economic globalisation and publicising what it perceived to be corporate abuses of democratic processes. Mike Moore, the then WTO Director General, commented: 'It's illegal and it's unfair' (in Meikle, 2002: 118). Shortly afterwards, on 1 December 1999, the WTO issued a press release stating that it is 'deeply concerned' about ®TMark's 'illegal and unfair' website. In the release Moore accuses the company of attempting to 'undermine WTO transparency' by copying the WTO website's design and using 'domain names such as "www.gatt.org" and page titles such as "World Trade Organisation/GATT Home Page" which make it difficult for visitors to realize that these are fake pages' (in ®TMark: 2005). Unsurprisingly, ®TMark's spokesperson Ray Thomas replied that, on the contrary, http://gatt.org/ is much clearer than http://www.wto.org/.

> Following any of the Gatt.org links – or reading any of the text – will make clear our interpretation of what the WTO is about, and that ®TMark is behind the site. Mike Moore must have a very low opinion of people to think they won't figure it out.

It is the WTO, according to Thomas, that is in fact misleading:

> They claim to be 'transparent' because their site includes thousands of official documents and the minutes of many meetings, but who could possibly have the patience to read any of that, besides corporate planners? All anyone actually sees is their bold declarations that they're 'delivering better living standards for everyone', or somewhat bizarre assurances that 'The WTO is not a world government and no one has any intention of making it one' [. . .] but the site doesn't even mention the violent riots in Seattle, London, etc., nor the reasons they're happening.
>
> (®TMark, 2005)

The site www.gatt.org (a reference to the WTO's predecessor, the General Agreement on Trade and Tariffs, or GATT) mimics almost every detail of the WTO's own site at www.wto.org, right down to the front-page warning about a fake site masquerading as the real thing. The parody site contains so many references to the WTO that search engines are directing people to it instead of the WTO's own site (see Figure 2.7).

®TMark, which claims to be seeking cultural rather than financial profit (ibid.) and uses corporate public relations techniques to publicise its successful projects to millions of people, aims to expose what it perceives to be undemocratic interests behind certain corporative powers. Appearing as The Yes Men, a small group of prankster activists led by Andy Bichlbaum and Mike Bonanno, 'interpreted' by ®TMark's Jacques Servin (who had intervened in the Sims computer game) and Igor Vamos, both also responsible for much ®TMark activity, they take on what they perceive to be corrupt corporations and institutions by impersonating them, through a process of 'identity correction' (The Yes Men, 2005), at conferences, on the web, and even on television. ®TMark, as well as The Yes Men, is not just creating performances *about* corporations, but rather *it is performing from within them*, thus quite literally contaminating, through artistic intervention, economic and financial production processes.

Figure 2.7 Yes Men Andy (left) and Mike attend the Heritage Foundation event. Later, they will interrupt a lunch with 600 other conservative delegates in order to propose a toast to Ed Meese (source: Courtesy of The Yes Men).

As suggested by Jean Baudrillard, 'the New World Order will be both consensual and televisual. That is indeed why the targeted bombings carefully avoided the Iraqi television antennae (which stand out like a sore thumb in the sky over Baghdad' (1995: 85). Hacktivists know that, without the media, they cannot make any difference, neither artistically nor politically, in the world of global corporate power because protest, in the twenty-first century, is first and foremost a spectacle of and about information. This is why to operate globally, to effect social change, it is crucial that companies intervene *within* the global world of information.

According to Hardt and Negri,

> The differences of locality are neither preexisting nor natural but rather effects of a regime of production. Globality similarly should not be understood in terms of cultural, political, or economic *homogenisation*. Globalisation, like localisation, should be understood instead as a *regime* of the production of identity and difference, or really of homogenisation and heterogenisation.

(2000: 45, original emphases)

Hacktivism is not only an objection to social homogenisation, but an opposition to the current regime of production. To express this opposition, hacktivism has to be active from within the regime of production for there cannot be identities that are 'in some sense *outside* and protected against the global flaws of capital and Empire' (ibid., original emphasis). Because communication, production and life form 'one complex whole' (ibid.: 404), resistance has to come from within, by means of contagion. This explains why '*the age of globalisation is the age of universal contagion*' (ibid., original emphasis). Because information, like land or capital, has become a form of property (Wark, 2004: 029), hacktivism has to reappropriate information. As suggested by Wark, '[t]he hacker class arises out of the transformation of the information into property, in the form of intellectual property' (ibid.: 036). Hacktivism is about the re-appropriation of the world of information and the spectacles that are generated by it.

According to the Critical Art Ensemble (CAE), power and capital have become increasingly nomadic and traditional forms of activism are no longer effective means of protest against capitalist and globalisation production processes.

> CAE reverses the familiar Deleuzian figuration which sees the nomad as the site of the Other, and insists that it is now *power* which is nomadic, rendering our social condition 'liquescent'. The only viable avenue for oppositional practice is to produce calculated 'disturbance' in the rhizomatic or 'liquid' networks of power itself.
>
> (Lane, 2003: 134)

Here, electronic civil disobedience performs, artistically, politically *and* economically, informatically, from within the world of information, acting principally at the level of the sign, performing through the modification of the meta-brand. This is where the possibility of change lies. As suggested by Baudrillard, '[t]he analogy between the terms "global" and "universal" is misleading. Universalization has to do with human rights, liberty, culture, and democracy. By contrast, globalization is about technology, the market, tourism, and information' (2003). So far, the primary artistic response to globalisation has come through hacktivism and its attempts to expose the fact that globalisation may be a privately conducted regime of homologation but, by penetrating its processes, artistically and economically, it is still possible to effect real social and political change.

3   City

The sign is more important than the architecture.

(Venturi in Venturi *et al.* 1972: 13)

Globalising the city

Over the centuries, villages gradually evolved into towns, towns into cities, and cities into metropolises, world cities, mega-cities, global cities and regional cities. Whereas the differences between villages, towns, cities and metropolises may be clear, partly because we have lived with these distinctions for a longer period of time, the specific features that determine the differentiation between world-, mega-, global and regional cities are still under discussion. Comprehending exactly how cities have changed and what they are in the process of becoming, however, is crucial not only to the understanding of the development of contemporary society, but also to the identification of the potentially revolutionary role that art can play within society. Moreover, the differences between mega-, world, global and regional cities will not only tell us more about how we live and make art, but also explain why generating art within an urban context may in its turn lead to some level of involvement with the wider mechanisms at the heart of political, economic and social globalisation.

So what are the differences between 'global', or mega-, world, regional cities and 'just' cities? Unsurprisingly, the first distinction is numeric. Mega-cities, and the same can probably be concluded about world, global and, especially, regional cities, indicate cities whose population exceeds eight million inhabitants (Fu-Chen Lo and Yue-Man Yeung, 1998: 7). However, the second difference is qualitative. Mega-cities are not only defined by their size, but also by their capacity to *perform* and *connect*. In fact mega-cities must be able to exchange and communicate productivity with other cities. In order to connect with other centres, mega-cities not only need ports, airports and teleports, but also an informatic and scientific infrastructure allowing them to become communication catalysts. This ability to exchange and communicate is a crucial feature of the mega-city and without it cities could simply not transform into them (ibid.: 10).

Some mega-cities have also been able to turn into world cities. The phrasing 'world city' first appeared in 1915 and was later revived in 1966 to indicate cities in which 'a quite disproportionate part of the world's most important business is conducted' (Hall, 1966: 7). Not only are these new types of cities of a certain size and capable of communicating and exchanging productivity with each other, as well as with other cities and towns, but they are also able to *act* as centres for world business. Distinctively, world cities need not just cater for the domestic market, but must be able to provide services for a world, 'global', market. Subsequently, world cities have to be capable of hosting headquarters of global corporations (Clark, 1996: 138) as well as office and convention buildings suitable for government. Perhaps unsurprisingly, world cities tend to have more in common with each other than with other cities of their own countries (ibid.: 139) and, again, it is not so much the size of their population, as the concentration of corporate control that distinguishes them from other, less 'global', centres of economic and political production and power (ibid.: 148).

In his review of this phrasing, Peter Hall had described world cities as

> centres of power, both national and international, and of the organisations related to government; centres of national and international trade, acting as entrepôts for their countries and sometimes for neighbouring countries also; hence, centres of banking, insurance, and related financial services; centres of advanced professional activity of all kinds, in medicine, in law, in higher learning, and the application of scientific knowledge to technology; centres of information gathering and diffusion, through publishing and the mass media; centres of consumption, both of luxury goods for the minority and of mass-produced goods for the multitude; and centres for arts, culture and entertainment.
>
> (in Fu-Chen Lo and Yue-Man Yeung, 1998: 17)

Not many cities are able to perform all these functions simultaneously. In fact, during the second half of the 1990s, only ten cities hosted the headquarters of nearly half of the world's largest transnational manufacturing corporations and of these, the top four accounted for the headquarters of nearly a third of them (Clark, 1996: 147). The top four also featured all the other characteristics of a world city. These figures illustrate how 'globalisation' is still very much a process in the hands of an economic and political elite and how most countries, though able to host capital cities and even mega-cities, are not necessarily capable of generating 'world' cities. This also suggests that world cities are such because of their capacity to *affect* the world, rather than their multicultural or intercultural qualities. Finally, this reveals a fundamental contamination between processes of economic, political, scientific and informational, but also *artistic* production. Like megacities, world cities are cities with a surplus, an *excess*. By working within the world city environment, and exploiting the hybridity characterising the relationship between these different production processes, artists are able to expose the links between economic, political, scientific, informational *and* artistic performance.

A number of world cities have been described as 'global' cities. Whereas some simply define these as cities whose citizens are from all over the world, like ancient Rome and Constantinople, for instance, used to be during the time of their empires' maximum stronghold and expansion (Cross and Moore, 2002: 4), others have chosen to define them not so much in terms of their cosmopolitan qualities but rather according to their politico-economic status. Saskia Sassen, for instance, notes that, whereas in the contemporary economic market production is increasingly dispersed, finance and services are being concentrated in fewer and fewer 'global' cities (1991). This process of separation between production on one hand and finance and services on the other has led to a distinction between sub-global and global cities. The latter, to impact globally, must be centres for financial services (banking, insurance) *and* headquarters of major production companies while *also* being seats of the major world-power governments (King, 1990 and Sassen, 1991, emphasis added). This shows that global cities are of a completely different order to other cities precisely because they are the *sites that initiate and control the production of globalisation*. In other words, the difference between mega-cities and global cities has to do with the global city's capacity to generate, control and propagate globalisation.

Interestingly, the production of globalisation requires global cities (note the plural) as a generative source. Sassen is clear on this process: 'national and global markets as well as globally integrated organisations require central places where the work of globalisation gets done' (2002: 8). Unlike other cities, global cities are therefore *'command points* in the organisation of the world economy' (Sassen, 2000: 4, added emphasis). They are 'key locations and marketplaces for the leading industries of the current period – finance and specialised services for firms' and 'major sites of production for these industries, including the production of innovations in these industries' (ibid., added emphasis). In other words, global cities are the 'factory' of globalisation. They are the economic, political, scientific, informational and artistic hub of the contemporary 'global' world economy.

Global cities exist only in their *interconnectedness*: 'there is no such entity as a single global city' (ibid.). Therefore, global cities need one another to ensure their respective political and economic survival. Moreover, in order to be interconnected, global cities must be informational and it is clear that 'IT and telecommunications networks are becoming, in a real sense, the very *sinews* of our globalising society' (Graham in Simmonds and Hack, 2000: 237, added emphasis). Thus, global cities are always also INFOcities, cities of and about information. To be able to communicate internationally, world, or global, cities have to be able not only to generate but also to regulate this flow of information (Clark, 1996: 156). This renders them *distinctive places for the gathering and dissemination of information* (Hall, 1966: 2). Whereas Manuel

Castells sees them purely in terms of this interconnectedness, '*flows, rather than organisations*' (1989: 142, original emphasis), networks rather than 'real' places (1997), Sassen shows that indeed they are networks but also *actual* places (2001: 349). The global city is in fact at once virtual *and* real. The surplus that characterises and defines it in terms of productivity, economically as well as artistically, is visible at both these levels and the excess is one of production *and* of the sign.

The global city is always intra-national. Not only is it international, or cosmopolitan (with first, second and third world present at once within it), but also it exists supra-, or, within the parameters of post-modernism, post-nationally. Again, Sassen is useful in explaining and clarifying the implications of this consideration. For her, 'the global city represents a *strategic place* where global processes materialize in national territories and global dynamics run through national institutional arrangements' (ibid.). In this sense the global city is not only the location that produces globalisation within a given nation, but also the generative and strategic headquarter of globalisation per se. So, as Sassen indicates, globalisation is not just a capital flow, or movement, but also 'the work of coordinating, managing and servicing these flows and the work of servicing the multiple activities of firms and markets operating in more than one country' (ibid.). In other words, globalisation, as well as the global cities that generate it, is at the heart of an economic and political capitalist social order of performativity. Although globalisation may be experienced as coming from the 'outside', it actually comes 'from the inside of national corporate structures and elites' and 'the global city is precisely the site where global processes can get activated *inside* a country with the participation of some of its national actors' (ibid.: 347, added emphasis). In this sense the global city acts as a stage, generating as well as exhibiting, producing but also performing globalisation. This stage, unlike a conventional theatrical stage, is not so much a mirror to the world, but rather it is able to generate worlds in its own image. And there is no outside – we are all always already inside this particular type of post-modern conurbation.

The global city is '*a function of a cross border network of strategic sites*' (ibid.: 348, added emphasis). And yet the interconnected global city, as Sassen indicates, 'is not simply a matter of global coordination but one of the *production of global control capacities*' (ibid.: 349, added emphasis). In other words, the global city is not only the factory but also the *regime* of globalisation. These new global cities, New York, London, Tokyo, Paris, Frankfurt, Zürich, Amsterdam, Sydney and Hong Kong, but also, increasingly, São Paulo, Mexico City, Bombay, Seoul, Buenos Aires, among others, (Sassen, 2000: 5) are 'strategic sites for the management of the global economy and the production of the most advanced services and financial operations' (ibid.: 21). Their reliance on government, workforce, telematics and globalisation, has led to a reshaping of the organisation of the economic space within them. This reorganisation has ranged from the 'virtualisation of a growing number of economic activities to the reconfiguration of the geography of the built environment *for* economic activity' (Sassen in Fu-Chen Lo and Yue-Man Yeung, 1998: 391). It has also led to international investment, especially in the property market (Sassen, 2000: 6), and a reconfiguration of urban life which has seen the core of the producers of globalisation (the workforce and the corporations) concentrating in the centre with the middle classes moving towards an ever-expanding periphery. The drift towards the outskirts, and the implied travel, to and from the centre, necessary to the functioning of the global city, has led to the formation of global regions, which, described by Sassen as 'urban agglomerations in peripheral areas', are the product of the success of the global city. The ability to move between spaces while remaining connected to the workplace is in fact a distinguishing feature of the global citizen. Global cities have propagated rhizomatically throughout large and interconnected geographical areas where it is possible to witness a 'significant concentration of offices and business activities alongside residential areas in peripheral areas that are completely connected to central locations via state-of-the-art electronic means' (ibid.: 112). Not only need offices stay connected with one another, nationally as well as internationally, but also the workforce must be potentially productive at all times, whether from their office or while on the move in the city, between places. This means that in the global city, or global region, the office worker is not just 'working' while 'at work' but also while travelling to and from their office. In other words, the entirety of the global region must function as a meta-office, always connecting, tracking and watching its workforce's 'global' productivity.

Just as globalisation marks the end of the nation state, it also marks the end of territory (Badie, 1995). As we have seen, global cities, and global regions, are characterised by their ability to redefine and produce globalisation in their interconnectedness with other global cities and regions. The fact that they are government headquarters is almost secondary to the fact that they must be able to generate globalisation alongside other global cities in other countries. This emptying out of national territory, to allow for the interconnectedness of informational, economic, financial and political processes is of course a fundamental characteristic of globalisation. Because of this, our cities are increasingly recognisable as global, INFOcities, or *media cities*, spaces for and of spectacle. In other words, freed from territory, though tied to actual productivity and performativity, global cities are both intra- and supra-national and, as media cities, they are always also both real places and fictional spaces. In this sense the global city is a location, a production regime, *and* its own fiction(s). When we encounter it, we always do so as a social (political, economic) *and* fictional (aesthetic) '(g)locality' (Robertson in Featherstone *et al.*, 1997: 40).

Unsurprisingly, just as the first signs of economic globalisation sieved through the world markets, world cities started to transform themselves into *global* cities. Symptomatic of this metamorphosis was a fundamental change in the urban environment: *the turning of architecture into information*. Already, in 1972, the architect Robert Venturi had pointed out that Las Vegas was a completely new city, *a city made of signs*. Within this context, the appearance of the screen as part of the architectural design was a symptom of the transformation of the city into a global, media city. Famously, the Pompidou Center in Paris, one of the few truly global cities, built in 1971–9 had also incorporated a media screen onto its façade and architects like Bernard Tschumi, Jean Nouvel, Jacques Herzog and Pierre de Meuron all used buildings as urban 'transmitters' (Imperiale, 2000: 22), disregarding the use of edifices as mere containers and privileging a more hybrid, intermedial functionality. While Jean Baudrillard denounced the architectural screen as an invasion of architecture by advertising (1988: 19–20), Bart Lootsma showed that this hybridisation had led to a 'contamination' of architecture not just with economics but also 'with other media and disciplines' (in Zellner, 1999: 11). This contamination, at once a symptom of the mediatisation *and* the globalisation of the cityscape, suggests that we always encounter the global city in and through its hybridity.

Knowbotic Research

Art practices interested in the growing complexity of the urban space as both a virtual and real place can allow for their work to reside at the crossing between informational and actual processes of urban flow. One of the companies which has operated most successfully within this field is Knowbotic Research, or KR + cF, which was funded in 1991 by the Austrian artists Christian Hübler and Alexander Tuchacek and the German artist Yvonne Wilhelm. As suggested by Stephen Wilson, its work consists primarily of 'investigations of the nature of information in the contemporary technology-mediated world' (2002: 83). For Knowbotic Research, '[i]nterfacing reality means intervene in reality' (Hübler, 1997). This understanding of electronic space as always already part of the real, has induced the company to present the idea of the 'global' as a set of virtually interconnecting localities. In its projects there is a constant interdependency between the world of information and practiced space and so participants, by altering the data flow, can influence the construction of other individuals' environments and subsequently affect their own presence and visibility within it. The interplay between the real and the virtual data flow is thus exhibited as a fluid process-oriented exchange within which the viewer can intervene in the dialectic interaction of the virtual and the real. Interested in 'nonlinearity, multidimensionality, acceleration, compression, multiple layers, poly-perspectives, multifunctionality' (Wilson, 2002: 837), Knowbotic Research claims that new technologies allow for the creation of 'non-locations' and 'mem_branes' functioning as 'zones of difference which generate confrontation and point beyond the cross-communicated indexical exchange of information' (ibid.). It is through these non-locations and mem_branes that individual viewers can enter the machinic and become part of a post-human, rhizomatic, 'augmented' global world.

Figure 3.1 Knowbotic Research/IO_dencies – questioning urbanity, Artlab Tokyo, 1997 (source: Courtesy of Knowbotic Research).

IO_DENCIES – Questioning Urbanity (1997–9), for instance dealt with 'the possibilities of agency, collaboration and construction in translocal and networked environments' (Knowbotic Research in V2, 1998: 186). The project looked at urban settings in a number of cities by analysing the 'force fields' present in particular urban situations and offering experimental interfaces that allowed for interaction with them (ibid.). The areas explored, during the different stages of the project, were Tokyo, São Paulo and the Ruhr region in Germany, all global regions, which were analysed through different systems. In Tokyo (1997), for instance, Knowbotic Research worked in collaboration with the local architect Sota Ichikawa to identify a number of 'zones of intensity' through which certain 'qualities of urban movement (architectural, economic, human, information, traffic)' were written into a notation system (ibid.: 188). These movements were then digitally coded and could be observed and manipulated through the Internet. In this way, 'the non-local topology of the network and the local socio-topology of the city were meshed together via an interface' (Broeckmann in Weibel and Schmid, 2000: 62) (see Figure 3.2).

In *IO_DENCIES*, Knowbotic Research transformed movement recorded from places like railways stations, markets, hotels and other similar public

Figure 3.2 Knowbotic Research/IO_dencies – questioning urbanity, Artlab Tokyo, 1997 (source: Courtesy of Knowbotic Research).

spaces into 'flow charts' that could be modified online (Mulder and Post, 2000: 141). The company claims that through these, it attempted 'to engage with the friction and the heterogeneity of the urban environment by merging the closed and rational system of digital computer networks with the incoherent, rhizomatic structure of the urban space' (Knowbotic Research in V2, 1998: 186). In this piece, the city is seen 'not as a representation of the urban forces, but as the interface to these urban forces and processes. Therefore, the city features not as a representation, but as an *interface* which has to be made and remade all the time' (ibid.: 192, emphasis added).

Global cities are characterised by their capacity to generate globalisation at a political, scientific, economic, informational and artistic level. They are also defined by their ability to allow for communication between these different sectors, locally and globally. This means that the production and distribution of information is really a defining feature of the global city, and the global city is such precisely because it is able to generate a surplus of information at all these different levels of production. In encountering the global city, and perhaps even more so the global region, we continuously experience this surplus as an *excess of information*. In fact the surplus is not so much quantitative as qualitative. In other words, the excess is not so much abundance as rhizomatic hybridity. The performance of the excess therefore allows for a contamination between these different levels of production. And it is precisely because of this contamination that art can really impact on society. The urban interface, Knowbotic's so-called 'zone of intensity', thus becomes the complex and turbulent place where art and society meet and signs explode into reality.

The spectacle of surveillance

The principal means by which the global city controls its own performance of globalisation is through surveillance. Due to improved surveillance technology, we are no longer placing elected and limited sections of the urban space under surveillance but rather 'surveillance cameras have *electronically extended* panoptic technologies of power, transforming cities into enormous panopticons' (Koskela in Holmes, 2001: 134, original emphasis). This marks another fundamental characteristic of the global city; its capacity of 'acting' as a control centre. In the global city we do not simply perform. Whether artistically or economically, we perform under surveillance. We watch and we are being watched. Our performance is someone else's spectacle.

Of course there is not just *one* 'Big Brother', but rather we are under surveillance by a number of different and not necessarily concomitant gazes. As an average citizen, it is difficult to know exactly who, or what even, is behind a given surveillance camera, and whether, for instance, it is operated by a public service, a private business, an individual or a group of citizens. Also, it is impossible to know whether an observation point actually corresponds to an eye. So we do not usually know if a camera is switched on, whether it is recording, or even storing our data. In some metro stations in Helsinki, for instance, what appear to be innocuous wall mirrors turn out to be 'windows' from which guards can observe and monitor the public (ibid.: 141). Here, we are told, is the evidence that global city forms are 'at the same time transparent and opaque. While everything (and everyone) under vigilance is becoming more visible, the forces (and potential helpers) behind this surveillance are becoming less so' (ibid.: 141). This suggests that, far from being simply a method for the monitoring of the application of law and order, the surveillance camera is a complex and somewhat 'enigmatic' object whose agency is difficult to determine precisely because it 'has no eyes but it has "the Gaze"' (ibid.: 151).

A defining feature of the global city, or region, consists of its ability to put its workforce under surveillance. To accomplish this task, it is not sufficient to simply watch over people. Data have to be analysed and stored effectively. They also have to be cross-referenced to other data. In other words, the global city has to be able to *know* everything about its workforce's performance at all times. This ability to continuously update

and cross-reference electronic information has transformed global cities into
'*super-panopticons*' (Poster, 1995: 69):

> vast stores of information that constitute as an object virtually every
> individual in society and in principle may contain virtually everything
> recorded about that individual: credit rating data, military records,
> census information, educational experience, telephone calls, and so
> forth.
>
> (ibid.: 89)

Here, Mark Poster claims, there is a clear loss of distinction between public
and private since 'everything' always takes place in the public eye and even
the smallest electronic trace can be transformed into complex information
about our lives (ibid.: 69). In these super-panopticons everything we have
ever done, achieved or maybe, in the future, also felt and thought, is stored
as information. Through surveillance the global city is able to interpret life
as information and so our lives *become* that information.

Because of the growing equation between life and information, what
matters in the long run is not so much the identification of who owns the
individual gaze behind the camera, as who owns the database generated by
it. As suggested by Poster, it is in fact the entity that controls the database
that really operates this super-panopticon:

> As a meaningful text, the database is no one's and everyone's yet it
> 'belongs' to someone, to the social institution that 'owns' it as property,
> to the corporation, the state, the military, the hospital, the library, the
> university. *The database is a discourse of pure writing that directly amplifies
> the power of its owner/user.*
>
> (ibid.: 85, added emphasis)

Databases are easily appropriated and exploited, politically and commercially. In 1989 the Thatcher government in Great Britain, for instance,
instituted a policy 'allowing officials to use DNA fingerprint tests on immi-
grant applicants seeking to prove they have relatives in Britain'. As a consequence of this, 18,000 tests were carried out. In 1991 Canada adopted the
same procedure. In the United States, during the 1990s, the creation of ID
cards linked to an electronic database was discussed that would have
included 'finger prints, voice prints, and DNA sequences' (Nelkin and
Andrews in Conrad and Gabe, 1999: 200). This again raises the question as
to who should own the data produced by surveillance. 'Increasingly it is not
doctors or public health officials who collect tissue samples for identification, but government, law enforcement agencies, the military, and immigra-
tion authorities. Private firms are increasingly involved as collecting tissue
becomes a growing business' (ibid.: 201). In other words, the global city's
ability to monitor its workforce through surveillance, and the subsequent

capacity to analyse and store relevant, commercially useful, information via the database, is not only used politically to ensure that the global city is maintained in good working order, but also commercially. *Our lives, our bodies even, stored as data, have become more 'valuable' than our lives per se.*

Surveillance is not simply reducible to the act of putting someone under surveillance. It implies their commercial and political exploitation. David Lyon shows how surveillance leads to the 'collection and processing of personal data, whether identifiable or not, *for the purposes of influencing or managing* those whose data have been garnered' (2001: 2, added emphasis). According to him, '[t]o make a call using a cellphone or to send an email may seem entirely innocent until someone traces your whereabouts and contacts you, using the traces that you left in the course of communicating with others' (ibid.: 2–3). Unbeknown to us, companies using the Internet collect data from our hard drives about which websites we visit, what products we look at or purchase, so that they can send us customised advertising (ibid.: 4). This storage of information does not only leave us subject to political or commercial exploitation but also makes us vulnerable to error. Thus, for instance, in February 1999 a routine online search at the University of Michigan Health System brought up what should have been highly confidential records with names, addresses, social security numbers, employment status, treatment records of its employees (ibid.: 1). At the same time in Canada, Air Miles collectors who registered online found themselves having free access to the personal files of 50,000 other registrants, including names, addresses, phone numbers, email addresses, type of credit card and number of vehicles owned (ibid.: 2).

Described by Anthony Giddens as one of four central institutions of modernity (1985), '[t]oday's surveillance extends far beyond the state, above all to the marketplace' (Lyon and Zureik, 1996: vii) but also, increasingly, to politics. The phenomenon, which is at the very heart of the 'capitalist drive for greater profit' (ibid.: 6), is a crucial component of globalisation (ibid.: 5) and thus a defining feature of our society. Yet, interestingly, it is the worker, rather than the work, that is under surveillance (Regan in Lyon and Zureik, 1996: 21). This is because, at least in the Western world, sales are as important as production. So surveillance is not only focused on our ability to perform, our physical and mental health being the driving force for most genetic screening currently utilised, but it also concentrates on our willingness, desire and ultimately ability to consume. 'The objects of surveillance can be performance, behaviours, or personal characteristics, and a variety of surveillance techniques are available for monitoring performance, behaviour, and personal characteristics' (ibid.: 23). Through surveillance the global city ensures that its citizens are constantly producing *and* consuming, products as well as information.

As Lyon shows, the global city has become an intensely regulated space. So much so that, according to him, the real world is increasingly resembling SimCity (Lyon, 2001: 52).

Urban experience involves the regulation of daily life. Myriad of checks are made to ensure that we are in the right place at the right time, travelling at the right speed or carrying the correct items. We are positioned, placed, directed and traced as we travel, buy, study, telephone, find entertainment and work.

(ibid.: 51)

In the global city, '[f]eedback loops ensure that knowledge of what we do in the simulated spaces is reappropriated – sometimes before we act – to anticipate our actions, channel our desires and constrain our deviance' (ibid.: 68). This shows that the global city is far more than the environment in which we live. It is an intelligent agency that is not just satisfied in watching and monitoring our behaviour but also needs to anticipate it and possibly affect it so that it can derive the largest benefit from it. By being the regime of globalisation, the global city is, almost literally, controlling our everyday lives.

Art is a formidable tool in exploiting and exposing the different interests at stake in surveillance. Julia Sher, for instance, has often worked with materials from the surveillance industry and in installations such as *Security Bed* (1994), by addressing the connections between performing under surveillance, sexually as well as theatrically, exposed the uncanny overlaps between commerce, biopolitics, performance art and the surveillance industry. Bruce Nauman, one of the first artists to work with surveillance camera technologies, showed long before, in works such as *Performance Corridor* (1969), how through surveillance the viewer may become an integral part of the work itself. Similarly, in *Video Surveillance Piece: Public Room, Private Room* (1969–70) Nauman showed how the viewer can only ever see themselves as mediated, incomplete, fragmented, subject to a partial gaze. In both cases we can see that at the heart of the process of surveillance is a powerful technology that is not only able to watch over and monitor our lives but is also capable of defining and potentially creating our identities and their memories. Not only do we perform under surveillance but surveillance is also increasingly a condition of performance.

Surveillance Camera Players

One of the theatre groups that has most explicitly experimented with the concept and practice of surveillance is the New York-based Surveillance Camera Players. Founded by Bill Brown in 1996, the group has achieved approximatively 40 performances, mostly in New York, but also in Holland, Italy and England. Surveillance Camera Players, which has affiliated groups in Arizona, San Francisco, Bologna and Stockholm, claim that surveillance cameras are 'a tool of social control' and 'the detectable presence of the camera in the workplace, in stores, schools, city parks, street corners, even coffee shops serves to remind the individual that s/he is a citizen of a surveilled society'. At the heart of the work of Surveillance Camera Players is the denunciation of the link between the world of information and corporate interest. So, the group claims:

> It is important to remind oneself of the relationship between the eye of the media and that of the corporate police state – for they are both the guardian of the commodity, however nebulous and ephemeral that commodity may become. As a tactic designed to point out the paradox of a system that turns the lens on a public that has been taught to place more importance on images recorded by cameras than images seen by their own eyes, we propose *Guerrilla Programming of Video Surveillance Equipment.*
>
> (Carter, 1995)

The players create silent performance scenarios that they then perform by using placards to a selected number of surveillance cameras and their audience (which consist of both the operators of the surveillance cameras and the occasional passer-by whose attention has been captured by the performers). To Surveillance Camera Players, the debate is as important as the performance itself because 'Guerrilla programming is production of an action, not consumption of a product' (ibid.). See Figure 3.3.

The group actively encourages the rhizomatic, and potentially global, proliferation of its work through the creation of affiliated companies, in the United States and abroad.

Figure 3.3 'God's Eyes on Earth', St Patrick's Cathedral, New York City, July 2000 (source: Photo courtesy of Surveillance Camera Players).

We encourage those who wish to become performers, but do not live in or near New York City, to form your own 'Surveillance Theater' group (you can even use the name SCP, if you like), *provided* that any group calling itself the Surveillance Camera Players cannot destroy, disable or do anything else criminal in nature to any video camera, monitor or system. If you plan to form your own SCP, please check out our How To Do It guide. We *discourage* you from 1) asking the SCP to come to your town or city so that people where you live can check us out; 2) coming to one of our performances with the intention of being a spectator or a spy; 3) attempting to get us to perform in any location that is not under video surveillance by real security guards or police officers; 4) offering to help design or improve the design of our website; or 5) attempting any commercial exploitation of our existence or activities.

(Surveillance Camera Players, 2005, original emphases)

The first work produced by the group was Alfred Jarry's *Ubu Roi* (1996). Characteristically, the piece was performed in front of surveillance cameras to a crowd of passers-by. Other works enacted by the group during the 1996–7 season included Samuel Beckett's *Waiting for Godot*, Eugene Ionesco's *Rhinoceros* and a special adaptation of *One Flew over the Cuckoo's Nest*. All performances were open to the public, who could either see the actual play or watch the group's video monitors displaying the work in its progress. Members of the group, watching the performances on the monitors as well as performing as actors, were also videotaped, alongside the audience, for the purpose of documentation. Thus in *Headline News* (1999), a double bill, following a piece by the Living Theatre, they 'held up a series of placards, including one with a huge CBS logo captioned WE WATCH YOU WATCH' while other group members distributed hand-drawn maps marked with camera locations and explained to the crowd that they, too, were being monitored (Surveillance Camera Players, 1999) (see Figure 3.4).

The group's ability to make art while exposing the complexity of the surveillance industry is remarkable. Not only is the dramaturgy of each piece interesting in its own right, but the performances also raise questions as to what is really being performed and for whom, i.e. who is watching whom and why, or even, who is documenting whom and why. By feeding art back to the camera, the players literally interrupt the camera's recording of everyday life and thereby sabotage its attempt to transform us from citizens to consumers. Characteristically, the group only performs under surveillance, as if to say that any discourse about and around surveillance can only take place under and through surveillance. Moreover, by interrupting the camera's recording of the global city's everyday flow of life, the group literally contaminates its performance of globalisation *through* artistic practice. In other words, without destroying anything, and simply by returning art instead of life to the camera, group members temporarily halt what often appears to be an inevitable and ineluctable process of commodification.

Figure 3.4 'It's OK, Officer', Manchester, England, June 2001 (source: Photo courtesy of Surveillance Camera Players).

The group identifies the camera not so much with the protection as with
the exploitation of the global city dweller. According to it,

> Thousands of security cameras in New York [129 in and around Times
> Square only] capture almost every move you make, from buying your
> coffee to taking your final steps home after a day at the office. But more
> cameras are being added constantly – about 30 per cent more each of the
> last two years, according to security experts.
>
> (Hamilton, 2004)

None of the cameras, the group points out, are in so-called 'high crime areas'
and, as September 11th and July 7th sadly demonstrated, 'surveillance
cameras do *nothing* to deter terrorists' but rather 'the new cameras
have mostly been going up in gentrifying or already-rich *residential* neigh-
borhoods, where video surveillance is "useful" only because it gets discounts
on insurance rates' (ibid., original emphasis). The work of Surveillance
Camera Players thus shows that the display of surveillance has become an
integral, yet highly problematic, part of the contemporary cityscape. In this
way, it draws our attention to the fact that to be *truly* global, a city has to
be able to put itself under surveillance, so that the more surveillance is
available *and* visible, the more the city is able to show off its own 'global'
productivity.

Unquestionably, surveillance is becoming increasingly present in our lives, so much so that we are beginning to interpret the presence of surveillance cameras as a sign of wealth or even success. Not only are we all gradually becoming familiar with surveillance, but we are also becoming more and more dependent on it, both politically and commercially. We are also beginning to use surveillance as a form of spectacle, televisually, as well as in our streets and buildings. And as surveillance technologies evolve, we have started to become more directly involved not only as the objects but also as the subjects of surveillance. According to Surveillance Camera Players, Big Brother television programmes are a symptom of this phenomenon. Moreover, the group points out, citizens are now encouraged in the United States 'to play detective' and use their

> cell-phones to surreptitiously take pictures of people who look 'suspicious' and then send these pictures to the local police and/or the FBI, who will use computers running face recognition software to see if they match any of the pictures that are stored in their huge and always-growing databases.
>
> (ibid.)

This suggests that the global city citizen is not only under surveillance but also, increasingly, actively participating in the surveillance of others.

The global city transforms us all into seekers and makers of information. In this world, where information equals money, not only have our lives become synonymous with the information that we are worth, but also, we might be told one day, this information may well be all that we are now worth.

Blast Theory

Blast Theory, led by Matt Adams, Ju Row Farr and Nick Tandavanitj, not only hybridises media and performance techniques in aesthetically challenging and complex ways, but also explores the 'social and political aspects of technology'. Their performances are always intermedial, contaminating discourses as well as genres. Drawing on 'mixed', 'augmented reality', primarily within an urban context, members exploit the dynamics of the *excess* produced by the interface of technology, life and art. Their work constitutes a complex interdisciplinary investigation of the aesthetics and politics of new media theatre. Here, 'questions about the ideologies present in the information that envelops us' (Blast Theory, 2005) become the very weapon through which theatrical practice can affect the informatic, scientific, political *and* economic discourses around us.

The investigation of the overlap between art and life was already informing the dynamics of their early piece *Kidnap* (1998). In this sensational precursor to Big Brother (ibid.), two volunteers were selected from a few hundred applicants and subsequently kidnapped for a period of 48 hours. The piece was very difficult to construct, not only aesthetically, but also legally, financially and politically. In a sense, *Kidnap* started *in absentia*, as an advert of something that could happen. The cinema trailer sounded: 'Have you ever wanted to be on your own for a while? Ever wanted to let someone else take control? Have you ever wanted to leave everything behind for a few days? [. . .] You will have the chance to be kidnapped.' Viewers then heard Adams's persuasive voice saying that for a small registration fee '[s]natched in broad daylight, held for a short period of time, you will be released unharmed. [. . .] THIS IS NOT A GAME. THIS IS NOT A JOKE. CALL 0800 174336 FOR DETAILS' (Blast Theory, 1998).

Finalists were chosen at random and put under surveillance. At this stage of the piece, the finalists were videoed and photographed, so two of them could be selected for the actual kidnap. Already, through surveillance, their lives had, in a sense, been 'kidnapped', to the extent that surveillance consists of the act of 'capturing' our whereabouts, for financial or political profit. Following this initial phase of observation of the shortlisted candidates, Blast Theory selected two 'winners' at random. On a chosen date, the performers then abducted their 'victims'. In the documentation, we can see how, hooded and tied, unable to move, a young man and woman, unacquainted with each other, were separately 'snatched in broad daylight' from a pub and a car respectively, and taken by a van to a safe house where they were put under constant surveillance for a period of 48 hours.

Meanwhile, online, the audience could monitor the kidnap. Through a live weblink, they could see the 'safe' house in which the 'victims' sat together in an isolated room with scarcely anything in it, except for a couple of mattresses on the floor. They could also see them being fed in silence, being made to drink with a straw through a hole in the wall, being escorted to the toilet, and being given a few, pre-paid treats, including a Tarantino-like dance that strangely but perhaps not unsurprisingly totally unnerved the kidnappers' 'victim' who had requested it in the first place. Interestingly, the audience and the performers were not the only people watching the act. A 'real' psychologist was also observing the victims, thus seemingly providing some kind of insurance that they were fit to continue in their own 'performance' of *Kidnap* (Figure 3.5).

The work was at once a kidnap, a performance *and* a scientific experiment. The hybridity between these different spectacular forms is visible in the victims' behaviour. Although they claimed that they never felt threatened or hurt, and maintained that they even trusted their kidnappers, they were also quite visibly disturbed by the piece and its dynamics of total relinquishment of control (ibid.). Interestingly, they were both in and out of control. Thus, they did appear to be *acting*, because they were under surveillance *and* because they were to some extent inevitably conscious of their own performance, but they also appeared to be *acted upon*, in that ultimately they functioned as an experiment, a theatre of science. This complexity was

Figure 3.5 Kidnap, 1998. Performance event with web transmission where online audiences could control camera angles. Sponsored by Firetrap and Dazed & Confused (source: Copyright Blast Theory. Photographer: Gregorio Pagliaro. Courtesy of Blast Theory).

caused by the coming together, in both surveillance and performance, of a number of factors. The idea of performing for another, while a third party was watching, captured the dynamics at the heart of surveillance which, as we have seen, are not so much between two parties (the surveillant and whoever is under surveillance) as between three (the surveillant, those under surveillance and the operator, or database owner). Moreover, this work was not only documented, it was continuously mediatised and every stage was only visible to the wider audience in its mediation.

Kidnap is a complex piece about urbanity and surveillance, but also about art and life, politics and trade, media and liveness. Already through its beginning, the 'advert', it is clear that we are dealing with mediatisation and simulation, and that art and life will not be distinct in this work. The ironic tone of the trailer, the music and imagery, juxtaposed against Adams's voice, created a sense of trustful expectation but also of challenge and possibly even need. Although it is suggested that there is no actual risk involved, a *real* kidnap is advertised. Moreover, like other company works, *Kidnap*'s structure is layered and has more than one beginning and ending. So the performance unfolds and this time its focus is on the observation of the potential 'victims' and the actualisation of a virtual kidnap, through surveillance, in its turn, consisting of the snatching of instants of the shortlisted candidates' lives. This moment raises complex questions. Who is the audience here? Is it the project participants? Or is it the ICA viewers? What actually constitutes this theatre? Who is watching whom? Then almost inevitably the *real* kidnap takes place. Except that this is also the moment when the performance becomes most displaced. On video the act of kidnapping looks at once strangely gentle and brutal, enacted and terrifying, performed and real. This stage is all about the displacement and disorientation of the 'victims' on the one hand and their placement, or situatedness through surveillance on the other. The more the victims are being watched (i.e. located), the more they become disoriented (i.e. dislocated). The more they are disoriented, the more we, the audience, enjoy watching them, because the real spectacle here is the drama of the progressive destruction and (re-)creation of their identities. Finally, following the hasty release of the 'victims', again documented by video, the piece culminates in a press conference – not a discussion with the audience, but yet another mediatised event, as if to say that it is no longer possible to witness anything *live*.

In *Desert Rain* (1999–2003) the company also successfully meshed the real and the virtual. Developed in collaboration with the Mixed Reality Lab at Nottingham University, the piece was one of the most complex and powerful responses to the first Gulf War produced within the sphere of theatrical practice. Inspired by Jean Baudrillard's *The Gulf War Did Not Take Place* (1991) (Clarke, 2001: 44), and constructed following computer game logic, *Desert Rain* can be seen not only as a comment on the war itself, but also as an exposure of the crucial role that technology played within both the making and the viewing of the conflict. Described as a mixture of 'performance, game, installation and virtual reality' (Adams and Row Farr in Leeker, 2001: 744), *Desert Rain* 'attempts to articulate the ways in which the real, the virtual, the fictional and the imaginary have become increasingly entwined' (Adams in Blast Theory, 2002). Exposing 'the fragility and interconnectedness of the physical and the virtual, the fictional and the factual' (Clarke, 2001: 44), the piece was constructed as a journey through a virtual labyrinth aimed at disorienting 'the body in a very corporeal way' (ibid.: 47).

As in *Kidnap*, the piece started with acts of dispossession and disorientation. The viewers, stripped of their belongings, were given a hooded black jacket and asked to identify their objective from a card with the picture of an unknown person. They were then led to six chambers where, by shifting their weight on footpads, acting as joysticks, they were able to move virtually through their avatars in an environment that was projected in front of them on a fine water spray, or screen. The deserted landscape contained two buildings. The first building held a map of the environment; the second was a cylinder with six doors leading to pictures of each of the visitors on their respective platforms – an environment which thus created a link between the virtual and the real (Adams and Row Farr in Leeker, 2001: 745–6); and finally a desert landscape, which seemed empty but in fact contained the viewer's targets. At this crucial moment in the piece the virtual environ-ment was unexpectedly penetrated by a real performer who slowly emerged through the rain screen to hand over to the viewer another magnetic card. No words were spoken and as quickly and mysteriously as the performer had appeared they would also disappear again, as if swallowed up from the world behind the screen. Rachel Clarke sums up this moment as follows:

> This momentary interruption of the game disrupts the telepresence experienced by the participant, for it fractures their solipsistic virtual engagement with the screen and points to the potential of something existing beyond the realms of the image. [. . .] It is therefore the per-forming live presence existing alongside the vitriol world that enables a critique of virtual technologies to be considered.
>
> (Clarke in Blast Theory, 2002)

The exchange of one card with another led to the beginning of a third phase of *Desert Rain* in which viewers found themselves in a vast underground hangar containing numbers, which were in fact estimates of Iraqi casualties.

Figure 3.6 Desert Rain, 1999. Interactive game, installation and performance. A col-laboration with the Mixed Reality Lab, University of Nottingham. Co-commissioned by ZKM Centre for Arts & Media, Karlsruhe and Contemporary Archives, Nottingham, in association with DA2, Bristol and KTH, Stockholm. Funded by the European Commission's Kaleido-scope Fund and Arts Council England with Lottery Funds (source: Copy-right Blast Theory. Photographer: Fiona Freund. Courtesy of Blast Theory).

This part of the game could only be successfully completed if all players reached the end of the corridor. Players who had reached this phase were therefore encouraged to help others who still had to find their target. Once the virtual world experience was concluded, the final phase of the performance could start. Having left the virtual world in a ritual act of purification by walking through the water screens, the viewers found that the narrow exit corridor was blocked by a large mountain of sand. Having climbed up and come down the other side they would find that they had reached the final room of the piece. This space, simulating a motel room, contained a television that could be activated by swiping the card obtained from the performers during the virtual game. By swiping the card, each viewer's target appeared on the monitor sitting in the very same hotel room that the viewers were in. At this point it became manifest that each of the six targets had their life changed by the war. All targets had been talking about their relationship to the events during the conflict and how 'real' it all felt (Blast Theory, 2000). However, even at this point it was impossible for the viewers to tell whether the targets were real or fictional, and in fact one of the characters, the actor, even spoke about the event as 'layer upon layer of simulation reverberating from every surface' (Clarke, 2001: 47). At no point did the piece offer a synthesis or clarification of its multilayered structure, thus suggesting that in today's society of spectacle it is no longer possible to tell the real and the virtual, facts and fiction apart. Upon leaving the room, the viewers could finally change back into their original clothing and then leave, still unaware that some time later, they would find something unexpected in their pockets – a small box of 100,000 sand grains reporting a quotation from a speech by General Colin Powell from the *New York Times* of 23 March 1991 referring to the possible number of Iraqis killed during the war: 'It's really not a number I'm terribly interested in.'

The very set of *Desert Rain* was a contamination of 'the real and the virtual, each mirroring the design of the other, and connected through the permeable and physically traversable rain curtain' (Blast Theory, 2002). As explained by Adams, here, just as in the case of the real conflict, 'the real penetrates into the virtual and vice versa' (in Leeker, 2001: 744). This hybridity and contamination between ideology and aesthetics, real and virtual, performance and life, was once again also perceivable at an ontological level. The space of *Desert Rain* felt immersive without being so. Nothing was what it seemed, and even the feeling of being free to roam in this land of desert and rain was in fact ultimately simulated by the control room operated by the company. As indicated by Blast Theory, '[t]he rotating world is "leaking" over to the fabric walls by "mistake" not by intentional design. On the other hand the feeling and experience is that one is completely surrounded by water, light, graphics and sound' (Blast Theory, 2002). Here, the clash between the liquidity of life and the fixity of the sign was reversed and while life was almost suspended, the immersive quality of the work distracting us from ourselves, signs here really could be taken for wonders.

TRUCOLD (2002), a piece about a global cityscape, consisted of a series of fixed camera shots of 'eerie, strangely depopulated, difficult to place, urban views: all of them at night, sometimes in glowing fog and set to electronic music' (Figure 3.7). Here, 'each location is illuminated by electronic light – security spots, street lamps and banks of unforgiving fluorescent tubes in empty offices'. In this seemingly unforgiving representation of the contemporary cityrama, we witness the urban space as a global place. By partially erasing 'the ephemeral passage of traffic and people', the work 'presents the urban fabric as monolithic, expansive and subject to minute shifts that might otherwise pass unmarked'.

Seemingly absent people are in fact present, but always as trace, on the 'margins': 'a running man appears as a blur, another is briefly reflected in a marble column' (Blast Theory, 2005). According to the company, 'the work also plays with the limits and effects of technology. [. . .] The act of image capture itself is bordering on entropy' (ibid.). In this controlled but also entropic space, the coming together of virtual and real, technology and fiction, politics and economics produces an excess of signification. So, interestingly, in *TRUCOLD* 'city locations such as these are not so much sites of urban alienation as places where something *ought* to happen' (ibid., original emphasis). Here, 'you find yourself trying to identify things, orient the space in the image, attaching real, imagined or fictitious events to it' (ibid.). This piece, which was shot by juxtaposing two cities, London and Karlsruhe,

Figure 3.7 TRUCOLD, 2002. Video. Created for the 2002 Biennale of Sydney, Australia (source: Copyright Blast Theory. Video Still from TRUCOLD. Courtesy of Blast Theory).

shows how the global city is always intra- and supra-national, a between-ness, in which the viewer can 'fictionalise their surroundings' and 'experience things which are not really there' (ibid.)

Subsequently, Blast Theory developed a series of performance games which, by exploring the fluidity of the game structure, allowed for the creation of mixed and augmented reality environments in which the company could, quite literally, operate its audiences. Through the game structure, Blast Theory could in fact exploit non-narrative structures and interactivity but also create environments in which the user was at once 'both inside and outside the game' (Adams, 2005). Thus for instance *Can You See Me Now?* (2003–5), winner of the Golden Nica (2003) at the Ars Electronica Festival in Linz, Austria, and developed in collaboration with the Mixed Reality Lab at Nottingham University, consisted of the interface between a virtual map and a real city, to which the map corresponded. In the real city there were real runners. Online, the players, who could operate globally, intra-nationally, had to escape the runners. The piece, which attempted 'to establish a cultural space' through technology (Blast Theory, 2005) was at once aesthetically and politically challenging. Not only did it allow for the co-presence of virtual and real, but it also showed how the virtual can indeed impact on the real. By means of surveillance technology, it also showed how the urban space is no longer *just* what we encounter in the city but also its mythology, fiction even, as well as the informational flow that at once locates, directs and defines us.

Adams describes the piece's dynamics as follows:

> I am sat online, playing in my bedroom, 2,500 miles away from where someone is on the streets of a city in the rain in an anorak and trainers, running as it gets dark through rush-hour traffic. And as I exert pressure with my index finger on the left arrow key and turn into the virtual park, this human being is required by the rules of the game to leap the hedge into the muddy grass and run up the steep slope through the park to maintain this game space.
>
> (Adams, 2005)

The piece which, not unlike *Kidnap*, explored 'the limits of our commitments and obligations to one another' and showed that 'electronic places are fraught places of trust' (ibid.) allowed the audience to see how the global city space is not only affected but directly manipulated by technology and how this technology not only allows for the complex layering of virtual and real, but also creates the possibility for one to impact on the other.

Similar dynamics were pursued in Blast Theory's subsequent piece *I Like Frank* (2005). The work was described as the world's first 3G mixed reality game using third-generation (3G) mobile phones which have broadband services and allow for high-speed data transmission and Internet and video links. Here, players in the real city of Adelaide could chat with players in the virtual city of Adelaide as they searched for the elusive Frank. The piece was again a mixture of hide-and-seek and treasure hunt (Adams in Blast Theory, 2005). When the real players and the online players came into proximity of one another, the online players could send text messages to the phones of the real players and the real players could record audio messages which were relayed back to the online players. Although, following computer game logic, 'Frank is an idea. You never meet him in person' (ibid.), the search felt very real and produced real effects.

Likewise, in *Uncle Roy All around You* (2003), also developed in collaboration with the Mixed Reality Lab at Nottingham University, participants were released into the urban space and told to find 'Uncle Roy'. After handing over their possessions, and in exchange for a handheld computer, participants were told to locate the mysterious figure in 60 minutes. The computer showed a map which corresponded to the game area. Meanwhile, viewers could monitor their progress and offer advice online by following the participants' actions through a virtual city map which was based on the real city's configuration. Here, in yet another challenge to the audience's trust, online players and actual players seemingly collaborated to find Uncle Roy. The real protagonist of this piece was the city space. Described as the 'arena where the unfamiliar flourishes', a 'zone of possibility' (Blast Theory, 2005), the city is in fact encountered here in its *excess*, as a bank of signification. To maintain orientation and be able to progress in the game, the viewer has to progressively decode the signs, work out what is life and what is fiction, trust one rather than the other and deal with the consequences of possible mistakes.

When I played the game in Manchester, whose geography is relatively familiar to me, I was under the clear impression that I was on a mission. Clutching onto my computer, I ran across streets, stopped strangers for directions and begged them for help in decoding my messages, never sure whether what I encountered was part of a fiction, the city's fiction, someone else's fiction, or even my fiction, or indeed part of the performance world created by the company, or *just* 'pure' life, encountered in its flow. And so, rushed by the messages, I found the park and the red bench, I sought the gaze of strangers and stared at the garbage abandoned in a narrow alley behind the Chinese restaurant, I followed the canal, looked at the windows and waited at street corners for someone to meet me. I also, at a later point in the game, thrilled by the prospect of my own success, entered a building block to find Uncle Roy's office, took a lift to the second floor, rung a bell and then, mistakenly, infiltrated someone's else's party. Panicked by the constant sense that I was running out of time, I convinced a group of total strangers who, it subsequently transpired, had nothing to do with Blast Theory or Uncle Roy, that I should answer the phone ringing in their office. Meanwhile, unbeknown to me, Nick Kaye, in the same building block, but on a different floor, had found Uncle Roy's *real* office. As a reward for the successful completion of the game, he was then put into a limousine and

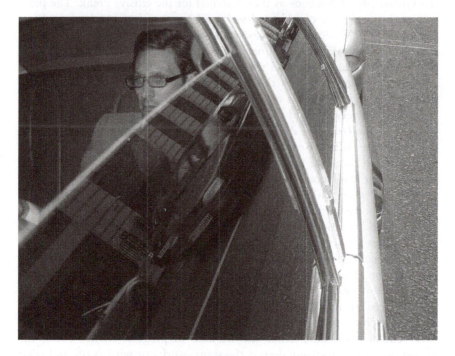

Figure 3.8 Uncle Roy All Around You, 2003. Interactive game played online and on
the streets of London using handheld computers. A collaboration with the
Mixed Reality Lab at the University of Nottingham and supported by an
Arts and Humanities Research Board Innovation Award, Equator, BT,
Microsoft Research and Arts Council England with Lottery Funds (source:
Copyright Blast Theory. Photo: Blast Theory. Courtesy of Blast Theory).

asked: 'Would you be willing to commit 12 months to someone you've
never met before?' Performance, just like globalisation, is all about trust.

When the piece was performed in London (2003), around the ICA, the
layering of fictions was even more complex. According to Blast Theory, this
was because the 'cultural, political and social ramifications of the site were
very well known to us'. In fact, in this case, the site was even more 'charged
with personal history', but also actual history since, apart from the historic
quality of the built environment, the piece took place at the time of the
Queen's birthday, and the site was crowded with police and surrounded by
helicopter units. The site was also the known location of a number of docu-
mentaries and films, the Harry Palmer films, in particular, and politics, with
the barracks nearest to Buckingham Palace being just round the corner
(Adams, 2005).

Whether in Manchester or London, however, being in this piece felt like
playing 'a Play Station game where the virtual characters and locations are
simultaneously real' (Churcher, 2003: 19). Like me, Stephen Armstrong

from the *Sunday Times* confesses that he was 'reduced to stopping passers-by and begging them for help, in the belief that they were Blast Theory stooges' (2003). Ultimately incapable of telling the fictions of history, politics, film, narrative, economics, apart from real life, the viewers, or players, of this game find themselves longing for directions. Unable to orient themselves without clear references from the game orchestrators, the viewers cannot but continuously reposition themselves in a world of flickering and deceiving signifiers. This is the spectacle of the global city, in which everything is made of information. Here, Blast Theory comment, there is a 'disparity between the city as a place of quotidian banality that's based around drudgery and servicing our various needs on the one hand and the city as a fantastic place for otherness and endless possibilities and where multiple worlds are nested in one another' (Adams, 2005). This disparity, or dialectic tension, between surroundings which are at once familiar and *unheimlich*, real and virtual, informational and material, continuously dislocates the viewers who through this process of *Verfremdung* are allowed a multiple perception of their own ontological position.

As in *Desert Rain*, the performers are not so much performing for us as performing us. By directly intervening in the interactivity, they directly influence what we see and how we see it. This is precisely where their work is most directly political.

> Thematics is one thing but the set of internal relationships in an interactive work is paramount and this is where the most fascinating things are going on and by not announcing a concept or theme so clearly you invite people to inhabit these spaces and then be implicated much more directly in the relationships that emerge and the ways that technology is mediating their relationships with other players and the artwork generally.
>
> (ibid.)

Not only have global cities become increasingly dependent on the mediatised, the virtual (Boyer, 1994, 1996), but also, through it, they have shown a progressive dematerialisation (Light in Crang *et al.*, 1999.: 120), a decreasing connection to their local geographies (Sorkin, 1992: xi), and yet an increased capacity to generate the 'hyperreal' (Baudrillard, 1995a: 12) and operate as fictions, *our fictions*. Blast Theory exposes not only this level of augmentation, or excess of the global city space but also draws our attention to the fact that, although we may be aware of the fiction, we do not necessarily know who that fiction belongs to. By continuously shifting our attention from fantasy to history, virtual to real, performative to life, Blast Theory radically exposes the powerful connections between the artistic, informatic, scientific, political and economic layers that form the global city environment in which we live. By operating at the level of the surplus, they create hybrid worlds charged with possibility, aesthetic *and* political possibility, of change.

4 Body

Whatever else it is, the cyborg point of view is always about communication, infection, gender, genre, species, intercourse, information and semiology.

(Haraway in Gray, 1995: xiv)

Scarring the post-human body

This is a 'somatic society' in which the body has become 'the principal field of political and cultural activity' (Turner, 1992: 12, 162). While the body is integral to our 'self-identity' (Shilling, 2003:1), and constitutes what we *are* in the world, it is also wrapped in aesthetic, philosophical, semiotic, sociological, biopolitical, medical, legal and economic discourses and practices, and so it is increasingly read as a map of dichotomous performative processes. Because of this fluidity between discourses and materialities, our bodies are unstable, changeable, even malleable. Now, more than ever, we are able to transform our appearance, alter our sex, acquire artificial limbs, mask the signs of our age, delay previously lethal diseases, and even predict and prevent the onset of some diseases altogether. One day, we may be able to move at a distance or regenerate parts of our bodies that have ceased to function. Although the body presumes an identity, we are striving towards the possibility of becoming at once multiple and fragmented. We live in a post-human world. We are seeking to become trans-human, possibly even transgenic.

Michel Foucault showed how the body is essentially under the influence of 'power' (1991). This is manifest at the level of discourse in that the body tends to '*disappear* as a material or biological phenomenon' (Shilling, 2003: 70, original emphasis). Thus the gendered body, Judith Butler proposes, 'has no ontological status apart from the various acts which constitute its reality' (1990: 136). This dematerialisation of the body, Chris Shilling comments, indicates that '*we have the means to exert an unprecedented degree of control over bodies, yet we are also living in an age which has thrown into radical doubt our knowledge of what bodies are and how we should control them*' (2003: 3, original emphasis). Through biotechnological intervention on the body, however, the influence of power is not only visible at the level of discourse but also in terms of the body's materiality. Not only can we write with and on the body but we can also, quite literally, rewrite the body. In many ways, the very centrality of the body in consumer culture (see also Featherstone, 1982) is at the heart of the body's fragmentation and dematerialisation, as well as its manipulation and control. Through globalisation, the body, already the subject *and* object of consumption, is thus also transformed into a product. In this sense, *the post-human body is a commodity.*

We know that 'bodies may be transformed and incorporated into organizational life through food and drink; organizational practices may be materialized into the bodies of workers; while the properties of food and drink may themselves be changed in interaction' (Valentine, 2002: 17). Since the biotechnological revolution allows for a rewriting, or remodelling, of the post-human body from within, the incorporation of the body into economic life has become more direct. The post-human body is part of globalisation's system of production. Part human, part machine, it is a means for the production of globalisation. Whether 'a phenomenon of options and choices' (Shilling, 2003: 3), a 'straight-jacket' or a performance 'integral to the exercise of agency' (ibid.: 193), the post-human body is an industry, as well as a commodity. It produces work *and* it is consumed, as a whole or in its parts. But the body is constituted by information, not only from a semiotic point of view, but also genetically. And whereas our legislative systems have tended to recognise that, to some extent, we are entitled to own 'our own' bodies, they have yet to determine who or what has rights over the genetic information that our bodies contain. Not only, as Shilling suggests, do we struggle to resolve who should own a transplanted body (ibid.: 4) but we also still have to acknowledge that, unless we create democratic systems to protect the information constituting our bodies, we will progressively succumb to new forms of global slavery through which life will become *Life*®™. *The post-human body is a site for legal dispute.*

The terrain of the 'post-human body' is unquestionably unsteady. Not only is the relationship between the human and the post-human body uncertain, but the question of who will be in control of the materialities and the technologies at the heart of its production is as yet unresolved. One of the fundamental characteristics of the post-human body is its ability to exist *beyond* the human. However, while the prefix 'post' indicates that the post-human comes after the human, i.e. that it is subsequent to the human chronologically, it also suggests that it is in the proximity of the human, in the sense that it still depends on the human ontologically. The closeness of this link is, of course, debatable. Likewise, the exact nature and power of the control systems that will determine the ethical implications of the growing separation between the human and the post-human is also an undecided factor. Unquestionably, the post-human marks a new fundamental development of what it means to be *human*. However, just as the post-human leads to revolutionary breakthroughs for the human species, whether in medicine,

society or art, it also prompts controversial and ethically challenging questions about what constitutes – legally, medically, philosophically and lin-
guistically – 'being human' in this global 'post-human' age.

One of the most interesting features of the post-human is its ability to act
as a cyborg. The literary ancestry of the cyborg, as Donna Haraway has
shown, is rooted in the liminal spaces produced by the West's regulation of
social and ethical 'norms'. Here, 'monsters' have been defining the limits of
community while implicitly challenging the boundaries of society in
Western imagination. So, Haraway explains, the Centaurs and Amazons of
ancient Greece established 'the limits of the centred polis of the Greek male
human by their disruption of marriage and boundary pollutions of the
warrior with animality and woman'. Likewise, unseparated twins and her-
maphrodites 'were the confused human material in early modern France who
grounded discourse on the natural and supernatural, medical and legal, por-
tents and diseases – all crucial to establishing modern identity' (1991: 180).
In both ancient Greece and early modern France, representations of 'monsters' have acted as indicators of the boundaries of the human. These ur-
cyborgs have not only worked as *other* to the human but also acted as a
terrain of liminality, experimentation, and possibly even subversion of the
social, artistic and political order. So the post-human has become first of all
a place of confrontation in which the human is faced with what it means to
be not-human, to be other-than-human. This confrontation, however, is not
one of opposition but rather of incorporation. In other words, *the post-human
is also not-human, other-than-human.*

Another interesting feature of the post-human body is derived from the
automaton. Norbert Wiener presented a history of automata that was
divided in four stages each corresponding to a specific concept of the body in
relation to the machine: a 'mythic Golemic age'; 'the age of clocks' (seven-
teenth and eighteenth centuries); 'the age of steam' (eighteenth and nine-
teenth centuries); and finally 'the age of communication and control' (1948:
50–1). Wiener believed that these stages generated four models for the
human body: the body as a malleable, magical clay figure; the body as a
clockwork mechanism; the body as a 'glorified heat engine' (ibid.: 1); and
the body as an electronic system. These characteristics of the automaton also
apply to the post-human. In fact, the post-human is often read as a mechanism, part of a larger networked electronic system, steered by an invisible,
unfathomable force. As shown by Arthur Kroker and Michael Weinstein,
the hypertexted bodies of cyberculture are not merely interfaced to the net,
they have 'become *nets* in their own right' (in Cavallaro, 2000: 29, original
emphasis). This means that *the post-human body is not only interconnected with its
environment, it is in itself a communication network.*

A third post-human characteristic can be identified in the post-human's
ability to assimilate robotic features. The robot, a figure which made its
debut in Karel Capek's play *R.U.R.* in 1923, marks the emancipation of
technology from the human. So with the robot, the machine became a plau-

sible alternative to, or even substitute for, the human, effectively marking the beginning of a post-human phase of production. In 1947, just over two decades after Capek's creation had come to life, the word automation first appeared at the Ford Motor Company (Huhtamo in Lunenfeld, 2001: 100) and a few years later, in 1955, Plantbot appeared, the first robot to be used industrially by General Motors (Giannetti, 1998: 8). Throughout the second part of the twentieth century, scary robots became friendly bots and automata were increasingly integrated into the methods of mass production, both culturally and socially. Like the robot, the post-human body is part of a chain of mass production. It is networked within the global markets. It is a workforce able to practice within a given set of performance indicators. *It is a system of production.*

The post-human is the space where the human confronts itself with and indeed incorporates the other-than-human. It is also the site where the systems of communication and control that allow for the post-human to function as an industry are located. In this sense, the post-human body acts as a transmitter, broadcaster of information. This happens semiotically, but also genetically. The post-human is prone to commodification. It is continuously driven to perform (economically, aesthetically, socially, etc.) and its value is often located in its capacity to perform more or less well. A space of discourse *and* materiality, the post-human body continuously reconstitutes itself between dichotonomous discourses. No longer ontologically stable, it is a body that must always express itself through performance (see McKenzie, 2001). Differently from the classical and modern body, the post-human body can be radically interfered with. This means the post-human body is no longer fixed, unchangeable, but rather that it can be rewritten like a blank canvas. Both signifiers and genes can be altered. *The post-human body is scarred.* Not only is it modifiable semiotically but also medically. Unquestionably, at once terrifying and sublime, the post-human body is already the most crucial and controversial site of aesthetic, biopolitical, ethical and economic dispute in the twenty-first century.

The issue of control is central to the figure of the post-human. This is because the new science of cybernetics, born in 1947 to unite communications theory, control theory, and statistical mechanics, is intrinsically about control. Even the actual word cybernetics was derived from the ancient Greek word for steersman (Wiener, 1948: 19). So, inherent in the concept of cybernetics is the idea of steering, navigating, which also implies the idea of a journey, or travel, and design, programming. The term cyborg was proposed by Manfred E. Clynes and Nathan S. Kline in 1960 to indicate how the self-regulatory control function of individuals could be extended to adapt to new (extraterrestrial) environments (in Gray, 1995: 31). Hence, the very term cyborg always implied the idea of control but also of otherness, of that which is not-human. In fact the world's first being named a cyborg was a white laboratory rat at New York's Rockland State Hospital (Haraway in Gray, 1995: xi). The rat had been implanted with a minute osmotic pump, which injected chemicals in its body at a controlled rate to alter its physio-logical parameters. This was the world's first organism in which the organic and the machinic had been perfectly welded, so that what had 'evolved' and what had been 'developed' were not for once colliding but in fact cohabiting in intriguing and yet seemingly perfect harmony. This ability to integrate organic and machinic, animate and inanimate, constitutes another crucial characteristic of the post-human. Whereas the human body is the process of a gradual and scientifically documented evolution, the post-human is the fast evolving and non-predictable product of a global biotechnological re-evolution. *The post-human body does not develop – it is developed.*

Because the post-human offers the possibility to transcend the human, it raises ethically complex and politically radical questions. As Haraway points out, cyborgs are 'the illegitimate offspring of militarism and patriarchal capitalism, not to mention state socialism' (1991: 151). They incarnate 'con-flicting visions of power and powerlessness' (Cavallaro, 2000: 46). They embody 'two opposite fantasies: that of the pure body and that of the impure body' (ibid.: 47). Thus cyborgs represent the ultimate human aspiration to freedom while simultaneously indicating its end as we currently know it. Implicit in the idea of the cyborg, and so of the post-human, is in fact not only its becoming other – animal, machine, environment, production process – but also the fact that there is an agency that is ultimately able to steer this process – Foucault's 'power'. The technology of the post-human, however, is not necessarily as dispersed as the post-human itself. In fact, the post-human, despite its advancement over the human, increasingly risks being dominated. *The post-human requires new systems of governance.*

Cyborgs have been defined as 'the melding of the organic and the machinic, or the engineering of a union between separate organic systems' (Gray *et al.* in Gray, 1995: 2); 'a self-regulating human-machine system' (Featherstone and Burrows, 1995: 2); or even any of us who either have an artificial organ (Gray *et al.* in Gray, 1995: 2), have been given artificial limbs or pacemakers, have been programmed to resist disease through immunisa-tion, wear glasses or hearing aids. Undoubtedly, with the appearance of the cyborg, the opposition between the natural (the biological, the organic) and the human-made (the technological, the artificial) that had underpinned philosophical and socio-political thought for centuries has irrevocably started to blur. Moreover, with the cyborg the opposition between real and fictional, life and literature has also started to fade. Thus for Haraway, for instance, '[a] cyborg is a cybernetic organism, a hybrid of machine and organism, *a creature of social reality as well as a creature of fiction*' (1991: 149, added emphasis). This means that the cyborg is not only a hybrid form, a collage of organic, biological and non-organic constituents, but that it is also a creature able to bridge the gap between the real and representation, between social reality and fiction. As Katherine Hayles suggests, cyborgs are 'entities and metaphors, living beings and narrative constructions' (in Gray, 1995: 322).

This capacity of augmenting the real through the fictional represents a salient feature of the post-human. *As post-humans, we are at once in social reality and in fiction – in the real and in the world of the 'spectacle'.* Thus through artistic performance, the mechanisms of economic performance that otherwise dominate the production of the post-human can be subverted. By operating at the level of fiction we really *can* effect social change. Despite its vulnerability, the post-human, already scarred at birth, commodified and controlled, can take advantage of its ontological ambiguity by turning economic productivity into aesthetic marvel. And herewith, the post-human, whose scar is also a sign of medical advance, whose commodification is also a mark of technological development and whose susceptibility to control is also a sign of society's increased ability to monitor itself, might finally be re-empowered to shape its own future not as an apocalypse but a wondrous genesis.

Stelarc

A theoretical and practical exploration of the post-human, in all its complex ramifications, is at the heart of the work of Stelarc, the 'foremost exponent of cybernetic body art' (Dery in Bell and Kennedy, 2000: 577). Stelarc has since his early suspension works experimented with the augmentation and extension of the body by using the skin as an interface between the 'inside' and the 'outside' of his body. Whereas in the suspension works, strings were used to challenge gravity and extend the body into space, the wires used in the later performances transformed his body into an INFO-body, a transmitter, or broadcaster of data. At once controlled by his audience and in control of his environment, Stelarc is a performance network, multiple, fragmented and dispersed.

For Stelarc the body is in fact an empty, hollow, container of technology: 'ONCE A CONTAINER, TECHNOLOGY NOW BECOMES A COMPONENT OF THE BODY' (ibid.: 563, original emphases). In this context, Stelarc claims, 'I went within myself' (in McCarthy, 1983: 15). What is encountered through this practice of excavation is not an unconscious process of thought but rather the *materiality* of the body. So, in *Stomach Sculpture* (1993–6), for instance, '[t]he idea was to insert an artwork into the body'. As the hollow body becomes 'a host' to the object (in Bell and Kennedy, 2000: 565), there were no longer any 'distinctions between public, private and physiological spaces' (Stelarc, 2002a). Here, '[o]ne no longer looks at art, nor performs art, but contains art' (Stelarc, 2002). In a reversal of the conventional understanding of inside and outside, Stelarc, thus brought the work of art, and subsequently the viewer, *inside* his body. The performance of Stelarc is not motivated by a psychological process but led by a physiological activity to which the audience becomes a complicit witness.

In *Event for Amplified Body/Laser Eyes and Third Hand* (1986) (Figure 4.1) Stelarc used fibre optics and lenses to demonstrate how the sensory and

Figure 4.1 Event for amplified body, laser eyes and third hand, Maki Gallery, Tokyo, 2
March 1986 (source: Photographer: Takatoshi Shinoda. Stelarc).

motor systems could be augmented through technology. The piece is an
interactive performance 'that controls, counterpoints, and *choreographs* the
motions of the virtual arm, a robot manipulator and an electronic third
hand'. The complex choreography 'combines real-time *gesture control* of the
Virtual Arm, *pre-programmed* robot scanning *symbiotic* EMG activation of the
Third Hand and *improvised* body movements' (Stelarc, 1997: 247, original
emphases). The viewer sees a variety of choreographed and voluntary as well
as involuntary movements, both from inside and outside Stelarc's body.
These affect the making of the external environment in which they themselves are immersed. In this sense the viewers are again both inside and
outside his body. In fact, the environment in which they find themselves is
quite literally designed by his bodily movements and stimulations. Through
this complex interplay of art and life, Stelarc presents his body as a medium,
able to transmit but also generate environments. For him, 'A BODY IS
DESIGNED TO INTERFACE WITH ITS ENVIRONMENT' (in Bell and
Kennedy, 2000: 562, original emphases). The body, he claims, 'BECOMES
A SITE BOTH FOR INPUT AND OUTPUT' (ibid.: 567, original
emphases). With 'constant reference to the body as a structure rather than a
psyche' (Stelarc in Featherstone, 2000: 138), Stelarc thus exhibits his body
as a medium *and* an architectural or environmental delimiter of space. The
communal act of witnessing Stelarc's performance work hence relocates the
audience within his own body. The body then responds to the stimuli of the

audience and thereby the audience is able to directly manipulate his body, even at a distance. This post-human spectacle illustrates at once how, within the context of the post-human, the individual body is always interconnected, performing in art and life, both an actor and a victim of a complex game of aesthetic and social biopolitical control.

Stelarc's work is unquestionably about fluidity and malleability but also manipulation and power. He acknowledges: 'I see these performances as architectures of operational awareness [in which] ethical, feminist or political considerations are allowed to unfold' (2002a). Thus, for instance, in *Ping Body* (1996) and *Parasite* (1997) this possibility of an interconnected play or game was taken a step further in that the artist's body was directly activated by the Internet. In *Ping Body*, described by Stelarc as 'an Internet Actuated and Uploaded Performance' (in V2, 1997: 27), the body in effect became 'a barometer of Internet activity' (2002a). Here, Stelarc linked his neuromuscular system to the net. The frequency and intensity of the pings drove his enhanced body and his neuromuscular spasms beyond his conscious control. For in *Ping Body*

> instead of the body being prompted by other bodies in other places, Internet activity itself choreographs and composes the performance. [. . .] The usual relationship with the Internet is flipped – instead of the Internet being constructed by the input from people, the Internet constructs the activity of one body.
>
> (Stelarc in V2, 1997: 27)

Interested in ideas about 'access and actuation, of hosting and of multiple agency' (Stelarc in Zylinska, 2002: 120), Stelarc reverses the usual relationship between the user and the net reducing the body to the status of a transmitter, a medium. Likewise, in *Parasite*, a search engine was constructed which selected and analysed images from the net and displayed them in Stelarc's video headset. The real-time images were then projected onto the body which was actuated proportionally to the incoming file sizes. In this work, 'the Internet is experienced more like a kind of external nervous system that optically stimulates and electrically activates the body' (Stelarc, 2002a). Here, we learn, 'the cyborged body enters a symbiotic/parasitic relationship with information' (Stelarc, 2002). In this work, as in much posthuman art, the body is always first of all generating, manipulating and broadcasting information. Moreover, the body can modify information but information can also modify the body. In other words, through performance, the information that constitutes the body can change.

Similar dynamics were also explored in *Telepolis* (1995) where visitors to the Pompidou Centre in Paris, the Media Lab in Helsinki and the Doors of Perception Conference in Amsterdam were able to 'remotely access and actuate' Stelarc's body in Luxembourg by using a touch-screen interfaced muscle stimulation system. Although the visitors thought that they were just activating Stelarc's limbs, 'they were inadvertently composing the sounds that were heard and the images of the body they were seeing' (Stelarc in V2, 1997: 23), hence authoring not only the performance of Stelarc but also again the very environment in which this took place. With Stelarc it becomes clear that '[o]ur skins no longer demarcate a line between inner and outer except in the limited sense of the body's endurance. What is generated within the body as information is hooked into global networks' (Poster in Zylinska, 2002: 28). The skin, thus representing the 'interface of the body with technology' (Stelarc, 2002a), becomes a fundamental site for post-human performance. As the 'place where boundary negotiations take place' (Benthien, 2002: IX), the skin or body surface becomes 'the place where identity is formed and assigned' (ibid.: 1). No longer the product of depth (the unconscious), identity is modelled as a dress, at the level of surface. Performing then, means 'scarring' the body.

In *Fractal Flesh* (1995) Stelarc again interacted with the net through an interface operating STIMBOD software, a touch-screen muscle stimulation system that allows his body to be moved from a remote source (Clarke in Zylinska, 2002: 49). 'Consider a task begun by a body in one place is completed by another body in another place' (Stelarc in V2, 1997: 19). This produced, in Stelarc's words: 'a body whose authenticity is grounded not in its individuality, but rather in the MULTIPLICITY of remote agents' (2002). In this piece, which created 'intimacy without proximity' (Stelarc, 2002a), the viewer becomes 'a parasite via the Internet [which is] safely hosted

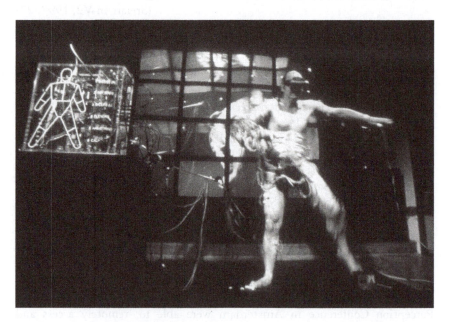

Figure 4.2 Split body: voltage-in/voltage-out, Galerija Kapelica, Ljubljana, 29 August, 1996 (source: Stelarc).

within Stelarc's body' (Grzinic, 2002: 99). Here, the viewer is able again to penetrate, *contaminate* Stelarc's body and modify it inside out. This work highlights how the post-human body is not only always interconnected, but also multiple, not so much without organs, as with an excess of organs. In *Fractal Flesh*, for instance, the artist's body is moved from a remote location. This means that one body may be activated by a number of agents, but also that one agency can have more than one body. The title of the piece of course highlights this potentially endless reverberation that is at the heart of the post-human body. This post-modern product is fragmented, multiple and rhizomatic. There is no one agency, but, again, agency is split, between discourses and materialities, performance and being.

Finally, for the project *Movatar*, Stelarc planned a reversed-motion capture system. Whereas motion capture allows a physical body 'to animate a 3D computer-generated virtual body to perform in computer space or cyberspace', in *Movatar* 'a virtual body or avatar [could] access a physical body, actuating its performance in the real world' (Stelarc, 2002). Thus here 'the body itself becomes a prosthesis for the manifestation of a virtual entity's behaviour' (in Zylinska, 2002: 129). In a reversal of the relationship not only between the inside and the outside, but also between real and virtual, Stelarc proposes to construct what has been described as 'a kind of viral life form which will evolve in its interaction with the body' (ibid.: 128). Thus the human can be altered both outside, via the use of surgery, and inside, via nanotechnology. Images, Stelarc suggests, can now be imbued with 'codes that make them more and more like viral entities'. These viral images 'have the potential for interaction and response', they can 'proliferate, replicate, and morph'. So, Stelarc concludes,

> there is the possibility that the realm of the posthuman may not simply be in the realm of the body or the machine but the realm of intelligent and operational images on the internet. Perhaps connected to a host body, these viral images may be able to express a physical effect and so the idea of a virtual and actual interface.
>
> (2002a)

For Stelarc, '[t]he body is obsolete' (in Bell and Kennedy, 2000: 562). Here, '[p]rosthesis is not something *added* to the self or even *used* by the self, it is quite literally *incorporated* into it' (Fleming, 2002: 102). Not only is the body always augmented, robotically, prosthetically, but it is also dispersed, networked, subject to multiple agencies. Yet this body behaves cannibalistically. It absorbs and consumes everything. It transmits everything. It becomes everything. And so, in watching him, in participating in his bodily activity, we too become part of the post-human performance of 'Stelarc'.

Body parts

The post-human body is malleable not only through sport and diet, but also via cosmetic interventions such as piercing, tattooing or even surgery. Marking or scarring the body has always had controversial implications so much so that already during Roman times tattooing was used to signal varying levels of political and social control (see Gustafson, 2000). Unquestionably (re-)writing the body was and still is a politically charged practice precisely because body modification represents both a means of controlling *and* subverting individual identities. Over the last few decades, we have become, as Mark Dery suggests, 'more than ever before, able to *remake* ourselves' (1996: 233, original emphasis). Because of this, Dery continues, the body 'is being transformed from a fortress of solitude into a combat zone' (ibid.: 231). Although in all probability the body has never quite constituted a 'fortress of solitude', in that interventions on the body date far back historically and are widely spread geographically, the degree by which individuals have been willing to quite literally rewrite their bodies is at once fascinating and disconcerting. In this sense, one might say, the body is becoming a 'combat zone'. Not only does it represent the biopolitical means through which individuals are transformed into a workforce, but it is also through the body that we are able to signal our acceptance or refusal of the culturally determined parameters of beauty, gender, ability, race, etc. that shape individuals into a society. Finally, it is the functioning of the body that affects whether we live or die. And therefore it is over the 'performance' of the body, i.e. over the appropriate functioning of its parts, that the most controversial and fraught over battles for the control of life itself takes place. So, who has a right to reproduce organs? Who own a body's (human *and* not human) organs? In what medical, financial and ethical context are we allowed to receive replacement organs? These are only some of the difficult questions that the reality of the post-human body prompts us to address as a matter of urgency.

Describing some well-known users of cosmetic surgery, such as the transsexual 'Tula' from a *Playboy* edition, or Roseanne, Ivana Trump, LaToya Jackson, Cindy Jackson from the *Jenny Jones Show*, who underwent more than 20 operations to make her resemble a Barbie doll, as 'morphs' (ibid.: 230), Dery draws attention to how the post-human body subjects itself not only to gradual but also drastic alterations based on what are often predetermined, pre-designed, synthetic even, paradigms of beauty. In fact, the post-human body is not so much remodelled because of health but rather by culture. It is now common practice for plastic surgeons to work with artists to draw up simulations, so that, as Sandra Kemp suggests, faces, or bodily features, are first generated digitally and then sculpted into clients' flesh (2004: 38). Surgeons are even asked by the medical textbook to acquire familiarity with classical art (Spitzack in Balsamo, 1999: 58). So the renowned Italian plastic surgeons Roberto and Maurizio Viel, for instance, practising at their Centre for Aesthetic Surgery in Harley Street, London, claim to use 'their aesthetic sense of beauty, together with surgical expertise, to create subtle improvements, which enhance both face and body, thus facilitating a rebirth of beauty' (2005). For them, as is clearly noticeable from their website, it is the history of philosophy and art, in society a well as in medicine, that leads their surgical work. First, there is 'beauty', then there are bodies into which the signifiers of beauty are to be carved. Beauty emerges out of a process of scarring.

Faces 'are thresholds' (Kemp, 2004: 40), zones of passage, prostheses even into the outside world through which we communicate and express ourselves in our everyday lives. We think faces are substantially unalterable. We still believe that once we are born with a certain face, we will also die with it. But through isolagen, a patented technique in which skin cells taken from one part of the body are grown in a culture to be injected into scars or wrinkles, we can now radically alter and even significantly rejuvenate our faces. In fact, with isolagen, new collagen is produced, which not only reduces scars or wrinkles but makes 'face transplants move out of the territory of science fiction to become an ever-increasing surgical possibility' (ibid.: 90). As examples of how processes of inscription and incorporation might work in the generation of a post-human future, Tim Lenoir suggests we look at the field of telesurgery in which 'surgeons work collaboratively with intelligent agent technology and surgical robots to perform complex procedures beyond the capabilities of earlier advanced surgical technique'. Thus Lenoir quotes a 'completely closed-chest endoscopic bypass surgery performed with a telesurgical system manufactured by Intuitive Surgical of Palo Alto, California' (2002: 220). Apart from the extraordinary medical potential, a surgery that leaves no scars, i.e. no recognisable signs or marks, also has potential ethical implications. Thus, for instance, we would no longer be able to *see* that someone has been operated upon. More worryingly, we might not even be able to notice that we ourselves have been surgically interfered with. In other words, the rewriting of our bodies is becoming increasingly substantial but also invisible at the same time. The already scarred post-human body hides its history. Though a palimpsest, a shifting and unstable textuality, it attempts to present itself as a blank canvas. In this sense the post-human emerges from a continuous process of *excess* but also *decay* and *erasure*.

Surveillance operators are increasingly relying on face recognition technology for the identification and control of the world population. It is likely that future identity cards, for instance, will be carrying information about our faces, and biometric security devices are of course already able to generate in-depth 3D facial portraits similar to holograms which can be embedded into the documents we need in our work and life. As Kemp notices, in the film industry, digital clones are often used for difficult or dangerous animations. It is in fact increasingly the case that simulations are utilised *instead* of human bodies. This practice, Kemp points out, could lead to misappropriation: 'who owns an image or a representation of a face? Is it possible to distinguish between representation and ownership (or private rights) of public or private faces? How are distinctions between use and ownership drawn?' The estates of Elvis Presley and Princess Diana, for instance, were both unable to place court bids to patent the deceaseds' faces and protect their estates from financial exploitation (2004: 131). Increasingly, we rely on avatars in science and in the entertainment industry. Shortly, we will also rely on them in office work interactions. However, we do not own our own avatars. In fact we neither own the data pertinent to them, nor the information they generate. And if these bodies of information can so easily be appropriated, modified, replicated, what will protect us from identity fraudsters? Who will own our avatars? Who will be acting in our name in virtual reality?

Lenoir describes how 'the ordinary bar code, the universal identifier for nearly every manufactured item on the planet', which today is still 'passive, registering information only when scanned by a laser that transmits the bar code's digital information', is to be enhanced so that it will 'actively transmit all sorts of data, a system called radio frequency identification (RFID) tagging' (2002: 221).

> An RFID 'tag' is a wireless semiconductor integrated circuit that stores an ID number in its memory and transmits that ID, as well as potential access to other information, through networked databases when accessed by, for instance, a Web browser. Standards have been agreed upon for manufacturing these devices, which are currently being produced at the size of 0.44 mm square, about the size of a large grain of dust. Hitachi Corp., for instance, is producing an RFID chip called the mu-chip. The mu-chip uses the frequency of 2.4 Ghz – the same as cell phones, wireless computers, and handheld personal digital assistants. It has a 128-bit ROM for storing the ID. Its unique ID numbers can be used to identify individually trillions of objects, with no duplication. Moreover, with a size of 0.4 mm square, the mu-chip is small enough to be attached to a variety of minute objects; it can even be embedded in paper. Manufacturing, distribution, and tracking systems can be built or enhanced using the mu-chip with an event-driven accumulation of, and on-demand access to, information stored in a database through the network.
>
> (ibid.: 212–13)

As information can be stored more and more imperceptibly, our life choices are becoming increasingly encoded. Thus information monitoring our eating, drinking, shopping, sleeping, learning, thinking, loving and training habits is becoming accessible globally. Through barcodes, our bodies are not only becoming part of, but quite literally being transformed into databases (see also Mary Flanagan in Mitchell and Thurtle, 2004: 168). This shows that the post-human body is networked in that it is rhizomatic and distributed, as well as globally accessible as information. Moreover, it is precisely because of its availability as data, that the post-human body is under constant global surveillance. It continuously transmits and receives data that allow us to produce and consume at maximum capacity. In this sense the post-human body continuously needs to monitor its own performance indicators. To do this, it no longer acts as a 'whole' but as an ensemble of parts. The post-human body is fragmented – *a body of parts*.

Organ trade is an example of how body parts are increasingly exploited commercially. While being unethical and illegal in most countries, organ trade constitutes a growing, extensive and lucrative practice. So, for instance, organs from executed prisoners in China, Asia and South America are used in commercial transactions for transplant surgery. In fact, according to Nancy Scheper-Hughes, 'virtually every site of transplant surgery is in some sense part of a global network' (in Fraser and Greco, 2005: 208). This is because there is

> a global scarcity of viable organs that has initiated a movement of sick bodies in one direction and of healthy organs – transported by commercial airlines in ordinary Styrofoam picnic coolers conveniently stored in overhead luggage compartments – often in the reverse direction, creating a kind of 'kula ring' of bodies and body parts.

Interestingly, 'the flow of organs follows the modern routes of capital: from South to North, from Third to First World, from poor to rich, from black to brown to white, and from female to male' (ibid.: 209). In the global economy the body is increasingly treated as a 'commodity' that can be bartered, sold, exchanged for money as a whole or in its parts (Scheper-Hughes in Scheper-Hughes and Wacquant, 2002: 1).

In a recent report on organ transplantation commissioned by the Center for the Study of Society and Medicine of the College of Physicians and Surgeons of Columbia University, it was noted that 'the sale of body parts is already so widespread that it is not self-evident why solid organs should be excluded'. The Bellagio Task Force, which investigated organ transplantation and then wrote the report, weighed a number of considerations and 'found no unarguable ethical principle that would justify a ban on the sale of organs under all circumstances'. Although the Task Force recommended that a ban 'on the sale of solid organs from live unrelated donors should be continued; at the same time, experimentation with (and close evaluation of) programs to reward families of donors of cadaveric organs should proceed'. The movement in favour of the commercialisation of body parts is steadily gaining strength, and so, for instance, the American Medical Association has already approved a proposal to establish a 'futures market' in organs from deceased people. The commercialisation of the body, the report notes, is also appearing under the guise of rewards for families that agree to donation. Hospitals, foundations, and private individuals are providing such families with compensation for burial expenses; the state of Pennsylvania recently established a fund to pay families of organ donors $1,000 for these expenses.

(Rothman *et al.*, 1997)

Thus the post-human body, alive or dead, as a whole, or in its parts, is increasingly treated as a commodity. It is tied to processes of economic, political and cultural globalisation. In fact, the post-human body is *a body that performs at all costs* (see McKenzie, 2001) because it has to continuously justify its own value. In this sense there no longer is a post-human 'body' – only parts, 'globally' rewritable, reproducible, tradable and no longer invaluable *Body-parts*®TM.

Orlan

A hybrid of art and life, Orlan, whose name represents an intertextual map of possible referents (Ince, 2000: 1–2), has, since 1990, undergone, a series of surgical operations, entitled *The Reincarnation of St Orlan*, to reconstruct her body according to a number of somatic and symbolic features drawn from the history of art. Thus her forehead is from Leonardo's Mona Lisa; her chin is from Botticelli's Venus; her nose from an unattributed sculpture of Diana by l'Ecole de Fontainbleau; her mouth from Gustave Moreau's Europa; and her eyes from François Pascal Simon Gérard's Psyche (ibid.: 6). Seemingly, Diana was selected because of her insubordinate and aggressive character, and because she had leadership skills, whereas Mona Lisa was chosen because she represents an emblem of beauty and because 'there is some "man" under this woman'. Psyche, on the other hand, was elected because she 'is the antipode of Diana, invoking all that is fragile and vulnerable in us', while Venus was opted for because she embodies 'carnal beauty' and finally, Europa because of her adventurous character and her capacity to look 'toward the horizon' (in Phelan and Lane, 1998: 320). Defined within these networks of literary and artistic references, Orlan exists in dialectical tension between insubordination and aggression, leadership and manhood, fragility and vulnerability, carnality and adventure. She is not a creature of unity but one of fragmentation. Hers is a post-human body of parts.

Everything about Orlan is artifice, from her name, Orlan, to her body, which remains a work in progress. She is not only 'a sort of living palimpsest' (Auslander, 1997: 131) but also that 'creature of social reality' *and* 'fiction' that Haraway describes cyborgs to be (1991: 148). In this sense, Orlan is post-human. Hers is an INFO-body, which is, quite literally, *performed*, modified in a theatre of science and *mediated* to global audiences. Her skin is 'treated as a fabric to be cut, shaped and stitched into a new look' (Botting and Wilson in Zylinska, 2002: 152) which becomes 'the place where identity is formed and assigned' (Benthien, 2002: 1). No longer simply delimiting the contours of her body, Orlan's skin has become her canvas, her screen, the very site of her aesthetic and political signification. Her scars are her performance.

Unlike Body Art, Orlan's Carnal Art is uninterested in pain and purification but rather presents the modified body as 'venue for public debate' (Orlan in Phelan and Lane, 1998: 319).

> When you watch my performances, I suggest that you do what you probably do when you watch the news on television. It is a question of not letting yourself be taken in by the images and of continuing to reflect about what is behind these images.
>
> (ibid.: 315)

In these works, as well as in her computer-generated images known as *Self-hybridation* (1998–9), in which her head is digitally hybridised with the 'head-sculptures, bone-structures, decorative prostheses and make up of Mayan beauties' (Ince, 2000: 87), Orlan once again reconstitutes her body as a site for inter- and meta-textual performance. Here, however, Orlan literally becomes a simulation. Her body disappears into the medium.

Through works such as *The Reincarnation of St Orlan*, Philip Auslander suggests, Orlan draws attention to 'the complicity of aesthetics, fashion, and patriarchy with the representational practices that define and enforce cultural standards of female beauty (e.g., painting, sculpture, surgery)' (1997: 131). Herewith Orlan effectively exposes the issues at stake in the cultural construction of beauty and shows that what we perceive to be *beautiful* is not so much naturally as culturally determined. Through surgery Orlan therefore does not so much succumb to, but rather, paradoxically, escape from, the dictate imposed by the patriarchal order. By reshaping her body not according to the current conventions of beauty but rather in dialogue with a number of parameters of beauty determined in different historical periods, under varying cultural and economic influences, Orlan exposes their tensions and highlights their contradictions. Here the excess produced by body modification is literally turned into a means of *resistance* to biopolitics precisely because it is utilised to destabilise notions of the subject as fixed (see Morgan, 1991). By using surgery to subvert her physiognomy, physique and even, to some extent, physiology, Orlan thus performs as a direct response to politically, economically, socially and philosophically determined aesthetic conventions of not only what a female body ought to look like but also of what art in general, or performance specifically, is intended to entail.

For Anne Balsamo, post-human reconstruction marks the end of the era of the 'natural' body and the beginning of the stage of the techno-body, 'a boundary figure belonging simultaneously to at least two previously incompatible systems of meaning – the "organic/natural" and the "technological/cultural"' (1999: 5). This new techno-, post-human body, as Haraway first suggested (1991), constitutes itself as a biopolitical response to past models of beauty, femininity and performance. Interestingly, Balsamo points out, '[t]he technological fragmentation of the body functions in a similar way to its medical fragmentation: body parts are objectified and invested with cultural significance' (in Featherstone and Burrows, 1995: 234). Far from constituting a sign of the post-human body's alienation, Orlan's body parts are invested with an excess of meaning. They are at once grounded in the history of aesthetics and hyperreal. They do not conform. In fact they are out of form. Because of this, they escape commercialisation. Their performance is *not* tradable. Orlan cannot be consumed.

For Balsamo surgically reconstituted bodies, or 'marked' bodies (in Featherstone and Burrows, 1995: 225) are at once in dialogue with materiality and culture.

> Cosmetic surgery is not then simply a discoursive site for the 'construction of images of women', but, in actuality, a material site at which the physical female body is technologically dissected, stretched, carved and reconstructed according to cultural and eminently ideological standards of physical appearance.
>
> (ibid.: 226)

By exposing the criteria by which cosmetic surgery takes place, and by exasperating its terms and explicitly naming its points of reference, Orlan turns sculpture into a live, time-based practice. The spectacle is the making of Orlan, a carnal art that exposes the modification of real flesh throughout a period of time. Carole Spitzack claims that cosmetic surgery deploys three mechanisms of control: 'inscription, surveillance and confession' (in Balsamo, 1999: 56). For her, the female figure is constructed as 'pathological, excessive, unruly, and potentially threatening to the dominant order. This gaze disciplines the unruly female body by first fragmenting it into isolated parts – face, hair, legs, breasts – and then redefining those parts as inherently flawed and pathological' (ibid.). Thus each part of the body, she claims, then becomes 'a site for the "fixing" of her physical abnormality' (ibid.: 57). Orlan utilises all the practices identified by Spitzack. Her performance text is written upon her own body. This writing takes place under surveillance, in the presence of the media, and confession is utilised as a means to convey the theoretical background that informs and inspires her work. In this sense Orlan's is a post-human feminist practice precisely because through the 'pathological, excessive, unruly, and potentially threatening' disruption of her own body parts, she turns the capitalist order of production inside out, and escapes the logic dictated by commercial performance indicators by offering herself as a truly unique, un-consumable product. With Orlan, scarred body parts are turned into aesthetic signifiers. *Life*®™ becomes art.

The augmented body: Kevin Warwick and Steve Mann

The post-human body seeks to become other than human. Augmentation is a primary means towards the achievement of this goal. Through its own expansion, displacement or even via an excess of organs, biological or synthetic, the post-human body is able to enhance sensory perception and become other. Moreover, the post-human body can reconstitute itself as a network of communication. In other words, it can share information with its environment, and interact with it. This expansion of the post-human body into its surroundings, so visible in Stelarc's practice, is also at the heart of the work of Kevin Warwick, Professor of Cybernetics at the Department of Cybernetics in the School of Systems Engineering at the University of Reading, UK. Warwick carried out a series of experiments involving the neuro-surgical implantation of a device into the median nerves of his left arm. This was to link his nervous system directly to a computer, which allowed for a number of human–computer interactions. As a cyborg, Warwick, like Stelarc, thus became the subject of multiple agencies.

In 1998, Warwick underwent an operation to surgically implant a silicon chip transponder in his forearm. The operation, carried out at Tilehurst Surgery in Reading, required local anaesthetic only. The experiment allowed a computer to monitor Warwick 'as he moved through halls and offices of the Department of Cybernetics at the University of Reading, using a unique identifying signal emitted by the implanted chip' (Warwick, 2005). The signal allowed Warwick to operate 'doors, lights, heaters and other computers without lifting a finger' (ibid.). This practice has obvious surveillance implications, since the computer is able to track and monitor Warwick's whereabouts. Through it, however, Warwick could actuate simple operations without having to use his own body to do so. Apart from the obvious benefits for disabled individuals, Warwick's cyborgian experiment shows how the post-human is increasingly integrated with his surroundings. Through the implant, Warwick in fact became part of a network of communication. At once human and machine, he was enmeshed in his own environment. The post-human relationship with space is one of continuous expansion.

The success of this experiment led Warwick to plan for a second implant. Thus in 2002 a 100-electrode array was surgically implanted into the median nerve fibres of his left arm (Figure 4.3). The idea was to look at how a new implant could send signals back and forth between Warwick's nervous system and a computer.

> The procedure, which took a little over two hours, involved inserting a guiding tube into a two inch incision made above the wrist, inserting the microelectrode array into this tube and firing it into the median nerve fibers below the elbow joint.
>
> (ibid.)

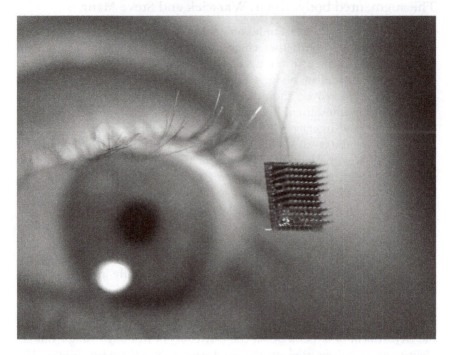

Figure 4.3 Interface Array consisting of 100 microelectrodes fired into the nervous system of Kevin Warwick to form a direct link between his nervous system and a computer and thus also the Internet. The link was bidirectional allowing Kevin Warwick to control technology directly by neural signals, to receive an extra (ultrasonic) sense and to communicate directly between nervous systems (source: Courtesy of Icube Solutions).

Following the operation, a number of experiments were carried out using the signals detected by the array. Most notably, Warwick was able to control an electric wheelchair and an intelligent artificial hand. Interestingly, the implant was also able to create artificial sensation. This means that sensation *could* be provoked virtually. In fact, according to Warwick, this chip implant technology 'has the capability to impact our lives in ways that have been previously thought possible only in sci-fi movies' (ibid.).

Interestingly, Warwick's implants could also hold personal information, 'from Access and Visa details to your National Insurance number, blood type, medical records etc., with the data being updated where necessary' (ibid.). Through such implants the post-human could therefore quite literally be transformed into a database for which the body would store information. This means that the post-human body has value not only because of the cost and productivity of its parts, but also because of the information it contains. Moreover, there is an increasing interest in the identification of possibilities through which the body could become an active, rather than passive, carrier of information. In other words, the post-human body might no longer simply be a databank but also a producer, maker of information. Thus the post-human body would be able to actively generate its own surroundings, environment, and even relationships. The post-human is also the space *between* humans.

Again, creating disturbing surveillance implications, this chip not only meant that a large amount of data could be stored on it, and so become 'globally' available, but also that a potential surveyor, a law enforcement agency, an employer, or even a parent could effectively track down its wearer's movements at all times. Although, this has potentially beneficial implications, it raises complex ethical concerns with regard to matters pertinent to individual freedom of movement and speech. It also, once again, raises the issue of who would control the surveyor and ensure that they act in bona fide and within the law. Finally, who would own the technology and the databanks that will quite literally lead us through our everyday lives? Who would own the information that *is* us?

A second implant was at a later point inserted into Warwick's wife Irena to allow for 'the investigation of how movement, thought or emotion signals could be transmitted from one person to the other, possibly via the Internet' (ibid.). In this case Warwick was interested in trying to address the questions 'how much can the brain process and adapt to unfamiliar information coming in through the nerve branches? Will the brain accept the information? Will it try to stop it or be able to cope?' (ibid.). Whereas the first implant identified him to the computer in his building, which opened doors and switched on lights when it knew he was nearby, the second implant linked his nervous system, by radio, to the computer and then his wife. This second implant allowed for 'remote control movements, extra sensory input, counteracting pain and new communication' (ibid.). Through this experiment Warwick was therefore able to link himself to a machine, and thereby acquire the capacity to operate upon his environment without seemingly doing anything. Moreover, by linking himself to his wife, he de facto became a plurality. This crucial work thus marks a fundamental characteristic of the post-human body. *The post-human is not singular but plural.*

Warwick, who believes that by 2100 we will 'see people able to communicate between each other by thought signals alone' (Warwick in Mackintosh, 2001) has attempted to establish a post-human system of communication that is no longer dependent on bodily functions. However, rather than rendering the body obsolete, these experiments show how the post-human body is such precisely because it is augmented, in excess, a 'borg'. The significance of Warwick's work is radical. Not only was he able to construct and successfully wear the 'first extra-sensory (ultrasonic) input for a human', but he also carried out the 'first purely electronic communication experiment between the nervous systems of two humans'. This means that Warwick was able to create the first post-human community, in which he was at once himself *and* an other. Two considerations can be derived from this work. First, because the post-human body is an augmented body, it is not a body that has left its past behind it, but rather one that is at once a palimpsest of its own histories and a gateway to those of others. In this sense the post-human body is not so much surpassing the human as incorporating it within other, larger contexts. Second, the post-human body is never alone. Not only is it always receiving information, as well as broadcasting it, but it is also always networked with its environment. In other words, the post-human body is in excess of information. It is also multi-human. So the augmentation is at once cyborgian, in that the post-human expands its senses through the machine, as well as 'borgian', in the sense that it could expand its knowledge by incorporating into its own those of others. *I will become us.*

Increasingly, cyborgs are associated with wearable computers. The idea that computers can be worn, that they should become part of the human everyday dress code, has been famously explored by Steve Mann, Professor of Electrical and Computer Engineering in the Department of Electrical Engineering at the University of Toronto. Throughout the years, Mann developed revolutionary, wireless forms of wearable computers which are almost invisible and which can be used to establish new, non-hierarchical forms of surveillance called 'sousveillance' (from the French *sous*, meaning 'below'), a term coined by Mann to suggest sousveillance's opposition to surveillance (from the French *sur*, meaning 'above'). Through wearable computers, Mann suggests, computer systems are able to share their wearer's perspective, 'much like a second brain – or a portable assistant that is no longer carted about in a box. As it "sees" the world from our perspective, the system will learn from us, even when we are not consciously using it' (Mann, 1997). With Mann's wearable computers the human body becomes enmeshed with its environment. Able to broadcast and record a personal viewpoint, they act in direct response to surveillance and thereby transform the citizen into an active receptor and transmitter of information. Through the wearable computer, the post-human body is in a continuous state of alert. At once present and absent, hyper-aware and dispersed, it lives in a state of excess and needs to learn to discern between what is relevant and what is not, what is programmed and what is real, what one chooses to experience and what one is made to.

Mann describes his wearable machines as

> a tetherless (*sic*) system that lets me roam about the city. I can receive e-mail and enjoy various other capabilities exceeding those available on a desktop multimedia computer. For example, family members watching remotely can see exactly what I see and, while I am at the bank, remind me by e-mail to get extra cash. Or I can initiate communication, using RTTY (radioteletype), to ask what else I should pick up on the way home.

This possibility of sharing one's everyday activities with other individuals, Mann suggests, could allow for 'a type of shared visual memory' (ibid.).

Moreover, it could create the possibility of an augmented reality in which the real *and* the virtual coexisted alongside each other. So, for instance, there are machines

> that can help us identify faces by comparing an incoming image to a collection of stored faces. Once the wearer confirms a match, the 'video orbits' algorithm that I developed enables the system to insert a virtual image into the wearer's field of view, creating the illusion that a person is wearing a name tag.

Wearable computers allow for a coexistence of fact and fiction through which the augmented reality in which we are immersed would be able to offer our senses a number of possible, potentially diverse and even contradictory, routes of information.

> Suppose that instead of just two people we have a networked community of individuals wearing computer clothing. This could be either a homogeneous community, all wearing the same form of the apparatus, or a heterogeneous community wearing several variations. People would most likely focus primarily on their own surroundings, but they could occasionally receive an image from someone sending an important signal. For example, someone anticipating danger might trigger a distress signal to others nearby over the Internet. Alternatively, the clothing itself could trigger the signal. For example, I have a heart rate monitor in my clothing and a footstep activity meter in my shoes. Heart rate divided by the rate of footsteps could register on a 'saliency index' that might warn of danger. If someone approaches you on the street, pulls out a gun, and asks for cash, most likely your heart rate would increase and your footsteps slow down, which is contrary to the usual patterns of physiological behavior. A community of individuals networked in this way could look out for each other much like a neighborhood watch.
>
> (ibid.)

Mann, who thinks we will become accustomed to clothing-based computing, affirms that this will

> blur the boundaries between seeing and viewing and between remembering and recording. Rather than narrowing our focus, living within our own personal information domain will enlarge our scope through shared visual memory that enables us to 'remember' something or someone we have never seen.

It is of course, once again, crucial that Mann's augmented, post-human, heterogeneous community is actually in charge of itself, and that systems are in place to make this a democratic process. It is also crucial that the post-human is ultimately able to remain in control of the information it broadcasts to itself. Otherwise, if we could be made to remember things we have not seen, we could be made to perceive experiences that do not belong to us. In this case we could easily become mere characters in the narratives of those who own the technologies that make the post-human body possible. It is unquestionable that technology leads us into the future. Though just how much our bodies really are 'led' is still to be seen. Mark Weiser of Xerox PARC, commenting on IBM computer scientist Tom Zimmerman's computerised shoes, predicts that some day customers walking into a store will pick up floorplan data from their shoes that will guide them to the merchandise they're shopping for (ibid.). This suggests that in the future advertising may take place within the clothes we wear. Because, through wearable computing, our clothes will become an integral part of our bodies, advertising will in effect become part of us. In other words, *globalisation will start from within the body.*

In surgery, systems that allow for an augmentation of the real are beginning to be in use. Lenoir suggests that

> soon surgeons will no longer boldly improvise modestly preplanned scripts, adjusting them in the operating room to fit the peculiar case at hand. Increasingly to perform surgery surgeons must use the extensive 3D modelling tools to generate a predictive model, the basis for a simulation that will become a software surgical interface. This interface will guide the surgeon in performing the procedure.
>
> (in Mitchell and Thurtle, 2004: 137)

This suggests that surgeons will more and more rely on virtual representations of the real flesh they are about to operate upon. Moreover, Lenoir notes that Charles A. Taylor and his colleagues from the Stanford Medical Center

> have demonstrated a system that creates a patient-specific, three-dimensional finite element model of the patient vasculature and blood flow in arteries then provides a set of tools that allows the physician to predict the outcome of alternate treatment plans on vascular hemodynamics.

Affirming that 'with such systems predictive medicine has arrived', Lenoir notes that here 'the surgeon is able to plan and simulate a surgery based on a mathematical model that reflects the actual anatomy and physiology of the individual patient'. Herewith, systems are used in which the model and the 3D stereo camera images are fused (ibid.: 143). In this sense the post-human body is always at once virtual *and* real, representation *and* flesh and blood.

In her study of the post-human, Hayles demonstrates that

> a range of developments in such fields as cognitive science, artificial life, evolutionary psychology and robotics were bringing about a shift in what it means to be human that differs so significantly from the liberal humanist subject it could appropriately be called posthuman.

Among the qualities of the liberal humanist subject displaced by these 'technoscientific articulations of the post-human', Hayles identifies 'autonomy, free will, rationality, individual agency and the identification of consciousness as the seat of identity'. The post-human, whether understood as a biological organism or a cyborg, 'seamlessly' joined with intelligent machines, is seen here as an entity able to participate in distributed cognition dispersed throughout the body, the environment, and possibly other bodies. Herewith *the body becomes a distributed virtual community*. Although agency still exists, it becomes a 'distributed function' (in Mitchell and Thurtle, 2004: 245–6) whereupon my body could become yours and 'I' really could become 'you'.

5   Animals and plants

Information wants to be alive.

(Thomas Ray, in Kember, 2003: 60)

The industry of nature

The end of the twentieth century marked the transformation of the animal into an 'anomal'. In the aftermath of technological and cultural advance, primarily brought on by computer and biomedical sciences, as well as postmodern aesthetic and political discourse, we have increasingly presented ourselves in terms of our post-human, post-operative, cyborgian qualities. We no longer talk about our *anima*, 'vital breath', but rather define ourselves as 'anomal', from *anomalus*, 'un-even', 'against, opposite to' 'regular' 'same', 'deviation from the common or "natural" order' (*OED*). Because of this departure from the normative, natural order, we have become increasingly obsessed with the possibilities of difference offered by structure, form, shape, aesthetics, skin/surface, dress and even spectacle (reality TV, for instance). At the same time we have started to define ourselves in terms of our genetic imprint. Hence our obsession with codes, databases, autobiography, surveillance. Because of our ability not only to intervene in our 'selves', but also to substantially modify ourselves, our animality is progressively turning into anomality.

This complex process has a number of implications. First, and most obviously, we are no longer describing ourselves in terms of our *anima*. In other words, we no longer wish to identify ourselves in terms of our 'vital breath', our 'being alive'. This is because we now perceive of ourselves as anomalous, i.e. as departing from the 'natural' norm or order of the 'human'. Through this we accentuate not only our *post*-human qualities, but also our ability to prolong life beyond life itself. Thus being post-human is no longer merely a descriptor of the fact that we are indeed alive (i.e. have a breath or anima), but rather a qualifier of our ability to stay alive beyond what, previously, could have been described as a point of death. Hence the post-human has started to delineate what could take us beyond our 'natural' life. Second, this process applies to both human and non-human animals. So it does not lead to an enforcement, as might have been assumed, of yet another classificatory separation between the human and the non-human animal, but rather a fluidity of kinds and species. In other words, *the post-human is also non-human*. In fact, often the post-human will be such precisely because of its ability to 'become animal', or, as we shall see, 'anomal'. Third, because the 'norm' that the post-human departs from consists of our genetic imprint, the process through which this departure takes place is one of modification or rewriting of the 'original' code at the heart of our anima, or life. This process is one of *performance*, not only because it is determined by an act of performance but also because, in this day and age, it is primarily influenced by performance indicators. In other words, the post-human anomal is categorised primarily though its ability to perform. In fact it exists exclusively because of its economic, rather than its intrinsic, value. Fourth, because the post-human animal, whether human or not-human, expresses itself in its performance, art and especially performance practice and performance studies, perhaps even more interestingly than ethics, are able to offer a critique of this phenomenon.

Animals are now, quite literally, designed by humans. This is primarily to satisfy a series of economic, scientific and indeed even cultural performance indicators. Through the act of genesis, code is turned into life – not a 'natural' life but a modified, anomalous life. Just as data are turned into flesh (see also Mitchell and Thurtle, 2004), these animals' flesh is increasingly detached from its 'natural' aura (the breath), thus turning them into a tool, prosthesis, even, to the human. These animals not only mark the modification of the animal into an 'anomal' but also constitute the key element in the evolutionary process at the heart of the transformation of the human into the post-human. Moreover, these animals only exist because of their functionality. They are the invisible, often monstrous, scapegoats of our society. Yet crucially, it is these 'anomals', with their new ontological apparatus, that will quite literally constitute the future of the human.

In *Humans and Other Animals*, Barbara Noske points out how environmentalists, especially in Europe, have been focusing on nature surrounding human settlements, thus neglecting domesticated animals which are thereby not quite 'recognized as nature' (1989: 2). Although domesticated animals are the most likely ones for us to encounter and, despite recent changes in UK legislation that make humans liable for their well-being, they appear to be a step removed from the natural order. Compared with other animals, which may even belong to the same species, but happen to live outside human settlements, they acquire, through their sheer proximity to the human, a different, higher, status. This signals an important shift in the understanding of the non-human animal phenomenon. Non-human animals, despite their physical being, are read in terms of their relationship to the human since 'their meaning is socially constructed'. In this sense *non-human animals acquire aura by being in the proximity or presence of the human*. 'Although animals have a physical being, once in contact with humans, they are given a cultural identity as people try to make sense of them, understand them, use them, or communicate with them.' So, '"[b]eing" an animal in modern societies may be less a matter of biology than it is an issue of human culture and consciousness' (Arluke and Sanders, 1996: 9). This reading of the non-human animal is interesting because it implies not only that the animal, like nature, to which of course the animal belongs, is in discourse rather than just 'out there', but also that intervening in the animal's proximity to and indeed relationship with the human has an actual affect on our reception of its animal, and, more specifically, anomalous existence.

Our understanding of the animal is framed by human discourse. And yet, one might think, the animal is also positioned in nature, i.e. it is part of a natural 'order'. As Donna Haraway has shown, nature, however, 'is not a physical place to which one can go', but rather a '*topos*, a place, in the sense of a rhetorician's place or topic for consideration of common themes' (in Shiva and Moser, 1995: 70). As a '*trópos*, a trope [nature] is a figure, con- struction, artifact, movement, displacement' (ibid.: 71). The position of the animal within nature, its location in relation to humans, its status, function and even value (nature, of course, also has a cost) are culturally, i.e. histori- cally, politically, economically determined. Moreover, whatever a given animal's classification, the sheer level of actual proximity to the human – precisely their difference, otherness, displacement – directly affect their aura and thereby determine the ethics of the human encounter with them. But the *topos* of nature is not fixed once and for all. And so, just as nature consti- tutes a variable set of parameters of placeness, the animal also, because of its determinacy, its *hic et nunc*, is continuously reconstituted and re-read as an *unstable* paradigm of the 'other than human'. Within this logic, the anomal is perhaps the most significant product of a fast-changing post-human understanding and practice of that technology that we call 'nature' (see ibid.: 85).

Throughout the latter part of the twentieth century we witnessed a significant progressive commodification of nature. So, for instance, as Haraway shows, classifications of kind and type have been denaturalised via proprietary marking through the patenting of transgenic and cloned organ- isms. While on the one hand nature has become denaturalised, i.e. techno- logically (re-)producible, commerce has increasingly appropriated both the realms of the 'natural' and that of technology in view of the possibility of producing its own 'nature'. As Haraway has shown, between the First World War and the early 1990s, biology was thus transformed from 'a science centred on organisms, understood in functionalist terms, to a science study- ing automated technological devices, understood in terms of cybernetic systems'. Likewise, just as biology was transformed from a 'science of sexual organisms to one of reproducing genetic assemblages', life science moved its focus from 'psychobiology to sociobiology' (1991: 45). As indicated by Sarah Franklin, nature becomes biology becomes genetics, through which life itself becomes reprogrammable information. This sequence proceeds along a path of increasing instrumentalisation, driven by commerce, legitimated in the name of public health, and regulated by the nation-state.

(in Franklin *et al.*, 2000: 190)

In other words, we can now not 'just' modify animals, but can actually *create* anomals. This must not be confused with the longstanding practice of husbandry. The verb to breed, as indicated by Franklin *et al.*, already indicates the act of cultivating, shaping, selecting and even artificially tending nature so that, for instance, '[t]he well-bred animal is the result of careful cultivation, selection and reproduction' (ibid.: 86). Breeding, like seeding, is of course a hybrid category, 'combining the natural and the cultural' (ibid.: 87). The anomal, however, is a more complex and revolutionary entity. Through the anomal, the human is not just shaping nature, but actually redesigning, reinventing it altogether. *Through the anomal, information becomes life.*

In Franklin's analysis, nature has been biologised and biology, in its turn, has been geneticised so that 'the geneticisation of nature and the facts of life have become inseparable from their instrumentalisation' (2003; see also Rabinow, 1996). As Noske notes, '[u]nder capitalism animals have come to be totally incorporated into production technology. [. . .] Animals produce wanted substances or serve as organic instruments in laboratories' (1989: 14). These animals are not allowed to socialise since most factory labour is taken over by machines and the 'animal has been removed from its ecosystem altogether' (ibid.: 19). Also, they have no contact with nature; they often eat food they do not tolerate and are separated from their own products (offspring, milk or even body parts). In fact, they are so alienated from their productive activity that their bodies are not allowed to improve and evolve. 'The *total* animal is being subordinated to this one activity. This one bodily "skill" which the animal is forced to specialise in, implies the extracting of one single part from a totality which *is* the animal. The animal is de-animalized' (ibid., original emphasis).

This new kind of animal, the anomal, exists only because of its economic and scientific value which is primarily dictated by the profitability derived from the trade of its parts. The anomal thus represents a departure from the technology of 'nature', a concept still indicating 'the *inherent* and *inseparable* combination of properties essentially pertaining to anything and giving it its fundamental character' (*OED*, original emphasis). Because the anomal has only value in its parts (and not necessarily as a whole) and because it plays no role in terms of its contact with humans, i.e. its actual proximity to the human, it has virtually no aura and is relegated as far away from our everyday lives as possible. More of an 'animal–industrial complex' (Haraway in Shiva and Moser, 1995: 85) than an actual animal, still able to eat, sleep, but also 'do nothing', the anomal's life only consists of 'working time' (Noske, 1989: 17). Not so much a companion or even, as Haraway suggests, one of 'the most extreme examples of domestication' (in Shiva and Moser, 1995: 85), but rather a tool, industry, production process, far away from the *domus* (house), the anomal constitutes the most destitute and alienated workforce of our society.

Pharming: 'anomal' and plant performance

There is a tendency to refer to animal rights in terms of animals that are most like the human (Tester, 1991: 14 and 46). There is also a tendency, as we have seen, to protect the animals we have had closest contact with. And finally there is a tendency to segregate laboratory animals from the gaze of society. Moreover, it is recognised that people find the use of, say, dogs and cats for laboratory experimentation morally less acceptable if they come from pounds or animal shelters than when they come from breeders or laboratories (Orlans, 1993: 209). It is therefore unsurprising that, since the 1960s and 1970s, researchers have consistently bred their own animals. In the UK, for instance, the number of animals used in research has been dropping whereas the number of transgenic animals increased fourfold between 1990 and 1995, with the actual production of over 215,000 animals. Far away from social scrutiny, these animals have, over the last 40 years, become progressively more anomalous to us.

Following the use of genetic modification in laboratories in the 1970s, a wide range of applications was put forward in the fields of agriculture, medicine and food production. The revolutionary potential of genetic engineering had quickly been identified by scientists and commerce alike. It is important to note that there are substantial differences between traditional biotechnology and genetic engineering practices. Although species were crossed in traditional biotechnology, these were much closer to one another than in genetic engineering where 'human genes have been put into pigs and genes from bacteria into plants'. Also, 'the pace of traditional biotechnology is much slower than in genetic engineering' (with the former operating within days, rather than years). Finally, whereas traditional biotechnology focused on species that provide human beings with food and drink, genetic engineering can design species 'involved in sewage disposal, pollution control and drug production. It also *seeks to create micro-organisms, plants and animals that can make human products*, such as insulin, and even, possibly, to change the genetic make-up of humans' (Reiss and Straughan, 2002: 5, added emphasis). In other words, not only are the gaps between animals and anomals potentially much larger than those separating different animal species from one another, but also the anomal's ontology is entirely expressed in terms of its ability to perform humanly programmed tasks. In this sense the anomal is the new workforce of the human. Life has become *Life*®™.

Genetically engineered mice and rats have increasingly been used as models for human disease. These kinds of anomals have been created to mimic specific diseases, which are the subject of research (ibid.: 169). The first such anomal was the Harvard/Dupont OncoMouse® developed by Philip Leder (patented 1988) at the Harvard Medical School. This mouse was bred to contain human DNA in the form of oncogenes that were able to produce cancer in each individual in order to provide standard animal models for the testing of pharmaceuticals. The mouse was marketed under patent as if it was a laboratory tool. In fact OncoMouse® was the first patented animal in the world. As Haraway suggests, it is 'many things simultaneously': an 'animal model system for a disease', 'a living animal', a 's/he', 'an invention', a 'commodity', and a 'machine tool' (1997: 79). Only five years after the OncoMouse®'s 'birth', in January 1993, there were over 180 applications for transgenic animals pending (ibid.: 98), and by the mid 1990s, David Winter, the president of GenPharm, made a remark making it clear that 'he considers the technique of custom-making a rodent so routine that he calls it "dial-a-mouse"' (in ibid.: 98).

In the same year, the SCID-hu mouse was developed by J.M. McCune and colleagues at SyStemix Inc, Palo Alto, California with a switched immune system that allowed for the study of severe immuno-deficiencies. This mouse was the result of transgenic engineering aimed at the production of a hybrid between a mouse and a human immune system, resulting in a mouse without its own immune system, but with a functional human immune system that could be used for the testing of pharmaceuticals. As in the case of the Onco-Mouse®, there was something of the human inside the SCID-hu mouse ('hu', of course, stands for human). Interestingly, because the OncoMouse®, like most other anomals, was modified at the germ line level, if the mouse was mated or even cloned, it could reproduce its modifications. Moreover, the OncoMouse®'s patent granted 'Harvard and DuPont the rights to *any* "transgenic nonhuman mammal" whose cells have been altered to make it susceptible to cancer' (Gray, 2001: 116, added emphasis). This of course exposes one of the paradoxes at the heart of the anomal's existence: despite being outside of nature, and having no direct value of its own (any individual little Onco-Mouse® only costs a few dollars), the anomal is able to generate significant capital for those who own it. In fact, the anomal is worth much more than any one animal precisely because it constitutes an entirely new species. Interestingly, this new species is able not only to work for the human but also to produce substances that only the human can otherwise generate. In other words, the anomal can be part of the 'global' human production system. At least theoretically, it could stand in for the human.

Cloning too, of course, has been a major instrument in the transformation of life itself into reproducible technology. The first cloned animal, Dolly, was created at the Roslin Institute in Scotland in 1996 (Figure 5.1). Dolly was cloned by utilising an adult cell from a six-year-old Finn Dorset ewe which was taken from a cryo-preserved cell line and transferred to a denucle-ated ovum of another sheep (Franklin *et al.*, 2000: 88). Shortly afterwards, in 1998, it was announced that a transgenetic ewe carrying human genes,

Figure 5.1 Dolly@grass (source: Courtesy of the Roslin Institute).

Polly, had been born, also at the Roslin Institute. Polly is both cloned and genetically transformed through the presence of the human gene. Subsequently, in 2000, scientists at the Whitehead Institute and University of Hawaii cloned over 50 mice which included Tetley, the 'first ever clone of clones' (Gray, 2001: 123). Through Tetley, the barrier between cloning and transgenics was crossed and Tetley represented the first mouse clone whose genetic material was modified in the laboratory *before* cloning. The first human embryos were cloned and then destroyed in 1993 (ibid.) and in 1997 a developmental biologist, Professor Jonathan Slack, and other scientists at Bath University created frog embryos with modified anterior–posterior pattern formations developed through RNA overexpression. The process, which raises the prospect of modifying anatomic features at embryonic level and growing non-human but also, possibly, human body parts is as follows:

> the early embryo is a sheet of similar cells with a group of special signalling cells at one end. The signalling cells emit a substance which forms a concentration gradient. The other cells respond to this by activating genes at different threshold concentrations. These genes encode transcription factors which are proteins that regulate the expression of other genes. Each body part in the embryo is 'encoded' by a particular combination of transcription factors. *If you alter the signal, or the combination of transcription factors, you can alter the anatomy in a predictable way.*
>
> (Slack, 2005, added emphasis)

In other words, what a being, whether human or non-human, will actually be, will not only depend on inherited or acquired features and behaviours, whether genetic or cultural, but also anatomical factors transformed or even produced in the biomedical laboratory.

Dolly's birth marked the beginning of a new era, culturally, politically and economically. To start with, Dolly was the first example of a mammal cloned from an adult body cell. In fact, Dolly was cloned using a nuclear replacement technique developed by the Roslin Institute and PPL Therapeutics PLC to test the suitability of different sources of cells for nuclear replacement. Interestingly, the six-year-old Finn Dorset ewe from which Dolly was cloned had long been dead. The shock at the announcement of her birth was such that it prompted former US President Bill Clinton to call for a worldwide moratorium on all cloning research and remind Americans, in a speech given on 18 May 1997, that 'science is not God' and 'our deepest truths remain outside the realm of science' (in Wadman, 1997: 323). Meanwhile, Ian Wilmut, Dolly's creator at the Roslin Institute, was alerting the world that, because Dolly had 'taken us into the age of biological control' (in Wilmut *et al.*, 2000: 17), 'life would never be quite the same again' (ibid.: 4). At the same time, Grahame Bulfield, Director of the Roslin Institute, was drawing attention to Dolly's 'tremendous commercial potential' (Roslin Institute, 1998), especially with regards to animal-to-human transplants and the understanding of diseases such as cystic fibrosis and arteriosclerosis. Similarly, Ron James, Managing Director of PPL Therapeutics, commented

> The production of transgenic livestock by nuclear transfer allows products to be developed far more rapidly and uses fewer animals than earlier methods. The technique allows us to develop therapeutics that would previously have been impossible or uneconomic. [. . .[For example, the large scale production of human albumin in the milk of transgenic cows for the treatment of burns will be cost effective only if the human albumin gene can be substituted for its bovine equivilent [*sic*].
>
> (ibid.)

Whatever one's beliefs, Dolly's creation unquestionably marked the beginning of a new era. Her viability was a sign of her complexity, not only as an anomal, but also as a brandable form of biocapital. Where Dolly was viable biologically because she was 'capable of life outside the womb', she was also 'viable in the corporate sense of a successful plan or strategy', and, finally, 'viable not only as a single animal but also as a *kind* of animal, a new species of what might be described as breedwealth' (Franklin in Goodman *et al.*, 2003: 96, original emphasis). Moreover, Dolly, like any other modified animal, was viable because she was a successful technology. Her anomality was the value of her wealth.

Although less known by the general public, Polly also represented a milestone in biotechnological research. She was the first transgenic sheep produced by transfer of the nucleus of a cultured fetal bibroblast which carried a human gene for blood clotting, Factor IX, that is used for the treatment of haemophilia. Because of her anomality, Polly was able to produce human Factor IX in her milk. Like Dolly, Polly represents a new species and constitutes a new kind of biological workforce. Like Dolly, Polly also constitutes a new form of 'biowealth' (Franklin, 1998) and finally, like other anomals before her, she carried a human gene, which again means that there was something of the human in her. One of the most fascinating and radical aspects of her life is constituted by the fact that she was transgenic. The technology at the heart of this process is potentially unlimited. Thus transferred genes, or transgenes, could be taken from any organism and transferred into others, so that, in principle, it is possible to transfer 'fungal genes into plants; mouse genes into bacteria; human genes into sheep' (Wilmut in Wilmut *et al.*, 2000: 6). This transference of cells, tissue or organs from one species to another, known as xenotransplantation, allowing for animal-to-human organ transplantation, alongside the ability to clone animals carrying a given genetic transformation, offers a therapeutic option for the hundreds of thousands of people dying each year of heart, kidney, lung and liver failure.

Transgenic experimentation also led to the development of pharming, through which therapeutically valuable materials, like proteins, are produced by genetically modified livestock, usually with human consumption in mind. In fact, pharming is constituted by the cloning of genetically engineered large mammals 'to produce things humans want', including human skin, cartilage, bone, bone marrow, organs for transplants, etc. 'A human woman modified so that her breast milk would include antibiotics will be, of course, a "pharm-woman".' Sheep could be engineered with an insect-killing gene from tobacco, salmon could contain chicken and cattle growth hormones, plants may be grown with freeze-resistant properties (Gray, 2001: 122). Pharming is of course a fast expanding and lucrative product of globalisation. In a report for the Organisation for Economic Co-operation and Development, Simonetta Zarilli reports that 'the genetically modified crop plantation has grown 35-fold since 1996, and the current estimated global crop area is around 60 million hectares, grown by almost six million farmers in sixteen countries' (Biological Resource Management in Agriculture, 2004: 29). This means that the transgenic crop area already covers 66 per cent of the Unites States, 23 per cent of Argentina, 6 per cent of Canada and 4 per cent of China (ibid.). Again, the revolutionary potential of this technology is substantial. Sir Liam Donaldson, Chief Medical Officer at the Department of Health (UK), and Sir Robert May's report 'Heath Implications of Genetically Modified Foods' describes genetic engineering as a process of 'cutting' and 'pasting' (1999: 6) and points out that the main differences between this and traditional animal and plant breeding is

i) Genetic modification enables single, well defined genes to be isolated and transferred, whereas with traditional methods many thousands of genes are 'crossed' at one time. ii) Genetic modification allows the introduction of a desired gene from one plant species into another. In addition genes can also be introduced from other organisms such as micro-organisms and animals.

(ibid.: 6)

The report, which also indicates that, although 'there is no evidence to suggest that the GM technologies used to produce food are inherently harmful', 'nothing can be absolutely certain in a field of rapid scientific and technological development' and subsequently there ought to be monitoring and regulation at an international level (ibid.: 3).

Despite its potential, xenotransplantation, as well as pharming, is still encountering substantial opposition, of which the following, extracted from Uncaged Campaign's website, is a typical example:

We are, literally, interfering with something we do not understand. What we do know is that pigs and humans both carry viruses within their genes and it is possible that these viruses could combine to create entirely new organisms. The public are rightly concerned about the possible health and environmental consequences of the genetic engineering of plants for food: now xenotransplantation threatens the integrity of the human body itself.

(2005)

In July 1997 *Nature* reported the growing concern for the welfare of animals used in transgenic work. A survey supported by the European Commission into public attitudes to biotechnology showed that most respondents considered the creation of transgenic animals, whether for research or xenotransplantation, 'morally unacceptable' (Masood, 1998: 311). Interestingly, the most successful aspect of the transgenic anomal is also the most controversial. The fact that the anomal can carry human genes, produce substances needed by the human species and act as a donor of organs for the human, in other words, the fact that it is not only useful to the human but it may actually become part of the human, makes it medically, culturally, economically and politically viable *and* valuable. Yet at the same time, this very act also contaminates what it means to be human and this, of course, makes it an uncanny if not frightening possibility. Unquestionably, the anomal marks the end of the era in which the human can be defined as entirely separate from the non-human animal. Not only is the anomal already human, in that it tends to contain human genes, but the human is also increasingly displaying anomal features. In other words, *the human is becoming anomal.*

Eduardo Kac

Since 1998, Eduardo Kac has been engaging with transgenic art, a form, he claims, in which 'the animate and the technological can no longer be distinguished' (2002). Its aim is the use of genetic engineering techniques 'to transfer synthetic genes to an organism or to transfer natural genetic material from one species into another, to create unique living beings' (in Stocker and Schöpf, 1999: 289). At the heart of this interest is the 'possibility of communication' between species (Kac, 2002). Whereas the scientists discussed in the previous sections of this chapter claim that scientific research, biomedical advance and commercial viability are the principal aims of their practice, Kac's interests are grounded in the aesthetic, social and indeed political connotations of his work.

Kac's most controversial piece *GFP Bunny* (2000) 'comprises the creation of a green fluorescent rabbit (named *Alba*), its social integration, and its ensuing public debate' (Kac in Kostic and Dobrila, 2000: 101). The GFP is a green fluorescent protein isolated from Pacific Northwest jellyfish which emits a bright green light when exposed to UV or blue light (Kac in Stocker and Schöpf, 1999: 289). The rabbit, Alba, constituted a new species in that she was inserted with the jellyfish gene and so, although she was completely white, she glowed when illuminated in a certain light (Kac in Kostic and Dobrila, 2000: 102). Kac defines Alba as a chimerical animal, in the sense of a 'cultural tradition of imaginary animals' (Kac, 2002) and perceives the project as encompassing the 'contestation of the alleged supremacy of DNA in life creation in favour of a more complex understanding of the intertwined relationship between genetics, organism and environment'. Kac, who also aimed at the 'integration and presentation of "GFP Bunny" in a social and interactive context', was encouraging the 'expansion of the present practical and conceptual boundaries of art making to incorporate life invention' (ibid.). For Kac, what was crucial in *GFP Bunny*, was not only the rabbit's actual creation, but its socialisation, its entrance into the public and, especially, domestic domain, in other words, its *becoming* a family pet, a bunny (Figure 5.2). Thus, Kac claims, '[t]he word "aesthetics" in the context of transgenic art must be understood to mean that *creation, socialization, and domestic integration are a single process*' (ibid., added emphasis).

To allow for a public viewing of Alba, Kac had transformed the exhibition space in Avignon, where the piece was meant to take place, into a 'cozy living room' that included a couch where Kac could live with Alba for a week in order to convey the idea 'that biotechnologies are on their way to entering our lives at the most basic level: in our private homes' (Andrews in Kac, 2002). However Kac's plans to domesticate the transgenic rabbit and thereby transform Alba into his family bunny failed when, shortly before the opening, the director of the institute that had engineered Alba refused to release her for public viewing (ibid.). This denial to exhibit Alba as an anomal forced Kac to reduce the piece to his own public appeals for her

Figure 5.2 Eduardo Kac, *GFP Bunny*, 2000. Alba, the fluorescent rabbit
(source: Courtesy of Eduardo Kac).

discharge and the promotion of her case through his website, further exhibi-
tions, talks and writings.

The piece, Kac suggests, was meant to stimulate a debate on the notions
of 'normalcy, heterogeneity, purity, hybridity and otherness' while also
showing 'consideration for a non-semiotic notion of communication as the
sharing of genetic material across cognitive life of transgenic animals' (in
Kostic and Dobrila, 2000: 102). The original plan was to remove Alba from
the laboratory of science and relocate her to a public art gallery. This
implied a process of both geographical and cultural dis-location whereby the
anomal would have been removed from its 'natural' laboratory environment
to be reinstalled in an 'un-natural' artistic environment as an animal. First,
Kac had planned to remove Alba from her secluded, undomesticated, life as
an anomal and instead offered her a life as an exhibit, not of science, but of
art. This would have implied that Alba would have ceased to perform as an
object of research and commerce, and started to perform aesthetically, as a
subject. Second, Kac intended to exhibit Alba in what was actually a reproduced (i.e. fake, not real) domestic environment, to show how transgenic life
was penetrating our (already culturally determined) everyday lives. Through
this act, Kac was not only reclaiming Alba as a pet but also as an animal
with an anima.

In theatre and performance art, the animal is often used to disrupt the
schemes of representation (see Giannachi and Kaye, 2002: 137ff.), whether,
as in the case of Societas Raffaello Sanzio, to 'suggest a pre-linguistic occu-
pation of the stage', an ' "anti-theatrical" presence in its resistance to and
evasion of the drama's rhetorical means', such as an 'inevitable *lack of technique*' (in ibid.: 150, emphasis added), or, as in the case of Motus's *Orpheus'
Glance* (1999), to indicate an 'ungovernability within the work' (ibid.: 195).
Thus the animal is used to introduce unpredictability, pre-discursiveness,
rupture or chaos. In *GFP Bunny*, however, the anomal, deprived of its
anima, cannot become animal and so cannot change. Not only is the animal,
absent from the title of the piece, which of course indicates not so much the
animal itself as its becoming, from GFP to Bunny (from protein to pet), but
also, like all other anomals, it was actually absent from the exhibition, thus
rendering Alba more of a media apparition than part of our everyday lives.

In discussing becoming animal, Gilles Deleuze and Felix Guattari point
out that 'becoming lacks a subject distinct from itself' and 'produces
nothing by filiation' (1999: 238). In other words, the act of becoming
escapes the product-obsessed capitalist market economy in favour of a more
fluid, process-oriented ontology. Because of the strong association between
Darwinian evolution and economic development, it is also possible to argue
that becoming escapes the processes of evolution. According to Deleuze and
Guattari, becoming is in fact 'involutionary' (ibid.: 238–9), moving between
terms, with a direction, but without the possibility of a catharsis. Thus
becoming is the prolongation of the middle, the paradoxical dream of the
possibility of not ending:

Becoming produces nothing other than itself. We fall into a false alternative if we say that you either imitate or you are. What is real is the becoming itself, the block of becoming, not the supposedly fixed terms through which that which becomes passes.

(ibid.: 238)

This 'involutionary' act of becoming, which allows for the possibility of a movement between terms, with a direction, but without a resolution, is at the heart of Kac's complex transgenic work *GFP Bunny*. Here, it is Alba's transformation from anomal to animal, i.e. her becoming animal, that is what we are meant to witness. Her involutionary and pre-discursive drama, her becoming, however, was not allowed to take place. In other words, her tragedy could not happen. Like other anomals, Alba was trapped in her theatre of science, unable to leave and thus ultimately unable to live (to breathe).

In discussing the etymological root of the word anomal/anomalous, Deleuze and Guattari refer to Georges Canguilhem's study *On the Normal and the Pathological* (1978: 73–4) in which '[t]he abnormal can be defined only in terms of characteristics, specific or generic; but the anomalous is a position or set of positions in relation to a multiplicity' (1999: 244). Thus the term 'anomalous', they point out, indicates the relationship between an individual and the multitude, drawing attention to 'a peripheral position, such that it is impossible to tell if the anomalous is still in the band, already outside the band, or at the shifting boundary of the band'. This suggests that *the anomal constitutes the liminal space of both the human and non-human animal*. Because of this liminality, the anomal, like the cyborg, is impure, contaminating and therefore unfit for domestication. Hence the anomal is hidden in the laboratory of science, publicly seen only through mediation (formula, text, video, photo, Internet). And yet because 'stability is assured in catastrophe by a *barrier*' (245, original emphasis), and because the anomal is in fact the barrier separating us from the unknown, i.e. protecting us from what one simply cannot be, the anomal represents the limit of what it means to be animal, whether human or not human, or, better, of what it means *not* to be animal, *not* to be human.

Unquestionably, the anomal, like the cyborg, also exists at the level of fiction, as a monster, chimera, marvel, centaur, sphinx, minotaur. Interestingly, the word monster comes from the Latin *Monstrum*, which in its turn is connected to *monere*, to warn (*OED*). Thus the monster is there to warn us, to protect us, but also to frighten us. Yet the monster, like the sirens, also lures us. As Elaine Graham suggests, the Greek term for monster, *teras*,

conveys something that is both abhorrent and attractive. The monstrous body is pure paradox, embodying contradictory states of being, or impossibilities of nature. [. . .] The monster is both awful and aweful; and insofar as the monster synthesizes taboo and desire, it further articulates its ambivalence for its creators.

(2002: 53)

In Graham's analysis, monsters therefore represent the

> demonstration of the workings of *différance*. Their otherness to the norm of the human, the natural and the moral, is as *that which must be repressed in order to secure the boundaries of the same*. Yet at the same time, by showing forth the fault-lines of binary opposition – between human/non-human, natural/unnatural, virtue/vice – monsters bear the trace of difference that destabilises the distinction.
>
> (ibid.: 54, added emphasis)

Deleuze and Guattari tell us that there are three kinds of animals: 1) what they call 'individuated animals', like family pets, 'sentimental, Oedipal animals each with its own petty history, "my" cat, "my" dog. These animals invite us to regress, draw us into narcissistic contemplation, and they are the only kind of animal psychoanalysis understands'; 2) 'animals with characteristics or attributes; genus, classification, or State animals; animals as they are treated in the great divine myths, in such a way as to extract from them series or structures, archetypes or models' and 3) 'demonic animals' 'pack or affect animals that form a multiplicity, a becoming, a population, a tale...' (1999: 240–1). Anomals have characteristics from all three levels and yet escape identification with any one of them. They are not only transgenic, they are trans-classificatory. They are the monsters of the new millennium, a property/pet (the Roslin Institute's sheep), a brand (OncoMouse®), an organ and even a food bank, safeguarding the future of the human species, a 'population'. They are both in our fictions, in our imaginary, as 'demonic animals', *and* they are out there, hidden away in the laboratories of science, setting the path to our future. They are both metaphorically and physically indispensable to the evolution of our society and yet they themselves are not allowed to evolve in their own terms. Reduced to the status of props, tools even, anomals are trapped in a human-controlled theatre of science.

Anomals may well work towards the end of famine, pollution, poverty, just as they may help to eradicate a large number of diseases in humans. And yet, as recently indicated by the *New Scientist*'s own Editorial a certain 'yuck factor', i.e. 'that visceral feeling that there's something wrong, even if you cannot say what' (2005: 5), has been preventing us not so much from believing in biotechnological experimentation, as from wanting to be in any way engaged with it. This 'not wanting to know' constitutes a dangerous position to hold which may have potentially devastating consequences. As suggested by Haraway, '{t}he global commodification of genetic resources is a political and scientific emergency' (1997: 62, added emphasis). In fact, some patents are so broad that they can give individual companies 'a virtual monopoly over the use of whole species' (Rifkin, 1998: 47). Geron and the Roslin Institute alone, for instance, control most of the patents and intellectual property associated with cloning. Moreover, it is acknowledged that cloned animals are often ill and of fragile health (Genewatch UK 2000: 2) and there are still no studies on the lasting effects of these technologies on human and non-human animals. It is also known that animal suffering and reduction of the gene pool represent a concrete danger for life on this planet. And yet 50 million transgenic mice alone are produced each year for a $200 million profit (Held in Mitchell and Thurtle, 2004: 271). It is therefore crucial that we continue to engage with biotechnologically produced or modified life forms legally, politically, ethically, philosophically, sociologically and artistically, so that economic performance could be turned into life performance, and the anomal object could reclaim, if only temporarily, its life as a subject.

The nature of Artificial Life

Etymologically, the word 'nature' indicates a birth, the beginning of the act of becoming. Thus, nature is genesis, life, as well as its constant transformation, its evolution. In *Contested Natures*, Phil Macnaghten and John Urry show that there is not a singular nature but rather various natures which differ from, and often contradict, each other (1998) in that they are produced 'by and through different social practices' (2001: 4). We cannot talk of a single nature but rather should think of a series of practices of nature which displace, contradict and even overlap with one another. Following the discovery of Artificial Life, it is now necessary to reformulate nature as encompassing not only a variety of cultural and social practices, but also what is un-natural, uncanny, technologically created, human-made. In other words, nature as an industry, a technology, includes its own artificial simulation. Thus, although being alive implies the presence of a *Leib*, or body (OED), it is less certain what *kind* of body is actually at stake in what is becoming an increasingly global industry of life generation. Artificial Life is not only part of nature, in that it resides *in* nature, but it is also an increasingly decisive factor in determining nature's becoming, its possibility to change and evolve. Through Artificial Life, our practice of nature therefore becomes more interactive and interventionist, allowing, for instance, for the possibility of a more or less immersive environment to develop all around us, through us and even because of us.

Christopher Langton, who first defined Artificial Life, showed that the principal assumption made in Artificial Life is that the 'form' of an organism can be separated from its matter, and that 'aliveness' is found to be a property of the former, not the latter (1989). Thus Langton claims: '[l]ife is a property of *form*, not *matter*, a result of the organization of matter rather than something that inheres in the matter itself' (ibid.: 41, original emphases). Artificial Life is in fact 'the study of man-made systems that exhibit behaviors characteristic of natural living systems' (ibid.: 1) and so '[w]hereas biology has largely concerned itself with the *material* basis of life, Artificial Life is concerned with the *formal* basis of life' (ibid.: 2, original emphasis). This means that there is a fundamental distinction between the study of biology and Artificial Life. Whereas biology has traditionally started at the top,

> viewing a living organism as a complex biochemical machine, and worked *analytically* downwards from there – through organs, tissues, cells, organelles, membranes, and finally molecules – in its pursuit of the mechanisms of life, Artificial Life starts at the bottom, viewing an organism as a large population of *simple* machines, and works upwards *synthetically* from there – constructing large aggregates of simple, rule-governed objects which interact with one another nonlinearly in the support of life-like, global dynamics.
>
> (ibid., original emphases)

By utilising Artificial Life models, it is possible to analyse not only how nature is formally organised, for instance, in terms of evolution, but also how both the concept and practice of nature can be operated and even modified by human intervention. In other words, through Artificial Life, it is not only possible to analyse what life itself is formally, but also to create intelligent natural environments that respond to us. So, far from representing merely a model for 'real' life, Artificial Life could become so much part of our understanding of life that it will be difficult to tell them apart.

Katherine Hayles shows that, conventionally, Artificial Life is divided into three major research areas: 'wetware', consisting of 'the attempt to create artificial biological life through such techniques as building components of unicellular organisms in test tubes'; 'hardware', consisting of the 'construction of robots and other embodied life-forms'; and 'software', consisting of 'the creation of computer programmes instantiating emergent or evolutionary processes' (1999: 225). Artificial Life software programmes with an artistic orientation have also been labeled as 'genetic art', following Peter Weibel's presentation of Artificial Life as art at the 1992 Ars Electronica Festival in Linz for works which simulate processes of life through technology (in Wilson, 2002: 56).

One of the earliest experimentations in which information was turned into 'life' was conducted by James Conway in the late 1960s and then transposed to a computer by Edward Fredkin of MIT in the late 1970s. This was the immensely popular Artificial Life game, *Game of Life* which consisted of a simple two-dimensional grid of cellular automata in which each position or cell could be in one of two states: on (alive) or off (dead). The spectacle of the game consisted in watching the immense number of permutations the game could adopt and the indefinite number of permutations that the 'game of life', just like life itself, could perform. What was unique about the game of life was its capacity to hypnotise the viewer into believing that the permutations they were viewing were not only 'alive' but almost choreographed – performed. The following passage sums up this realisation as follows when you programme the game on a computer and start the clock running, something amazing happens [. . .] Order is created out of randomness. Static, oscillating, and traveling patterns form from the primordial goo. Pattern interacts with pattern, spawning both higher-level patterns and randomness. But this randomness is food for another generation, and on and on the dance continues.

(Karakotsios, 1993)

A different kind of evolutionary spectacle was created in Biosphere II, described as the 'model for the living environment of tomorrow' (Röetzer in Beckmann, 1998: 134). Here, although the life created was 'real' rather than artificial, it was only being sustained through the artificial systems maintained by the computer technology that made the immersive environment possible. The equation between life and information also implies the possibility of simulating life virtually, as was the case in Char Davies's *Osmose* (1995) (see Figure 5.3), an immersive interactive virtual reality environment installation in which the viewer, fitted with a headmounted VR display and real-time motion tracking based on breathing and balance, could wander through what has been described as 'a sequence of "phosphorescent" spaces – the Grid, the Clearing, the Forest, the Leaf, the Pond – a garden of light

Figure 5.3 Tree Pond. Digital frame captured in real time through HMD (Head Mounted Display) during live performance of the immersive virtual environment Osmose (1995) (source: Courtesy of Char Davies).

framed by "stands of softly glowing, semitransparent trees" ' (Campanella in Goldberg, 2000: 37) (see Figure 5.4).

The equation between life and information also allows for an interchange between a given real ecosystem and information technology. So, for instance, a well-known example of a telepresent garden is Ken Goldberg and Joe Santarromana's *The Telegarden* (1994) which consists of a portable garden at the Ars Electronica Centre at Linz containing an industrial robotic arm that is controlled by the web and allows remote participants to plant seeds and water the plants created in the garden. This garden, like the other more or less 'real' natural environments described above, was not merely constituted by the gardens themselves but also by their capacity for changing and evolving. So what all these games of life have in common is their capacity for transforming, renewing themselves – their skill of being able to become.

A well-known example of genetic art is Karl Sims's *Galápagos* (1997) (Figure 5.5) in which virtual life forms, which have three-dimensional bodies with their own size, colour, shape, motion and articulated parts, as well as unique behaviours, are both 'artificial in their sharp-edged geometry yet thoroughly lifelike in their movements'. *Galápagos* consisted of 12

Figure 5.4 The Telegarden 1995–ongoing, networked robot installation at Ars Electronica Museum, Austria, http://telegarden.aec.at. Co-directors: Ken Goldberg and Joseph Santarromana. Project team: George Bekey, Steven Gentner, Rosemary Morris, Carl Sutter, Jeff Wiegley, Erich Berger (source: Photo by Robert Wedemeyer. Courtesy of Ken Goldberg).

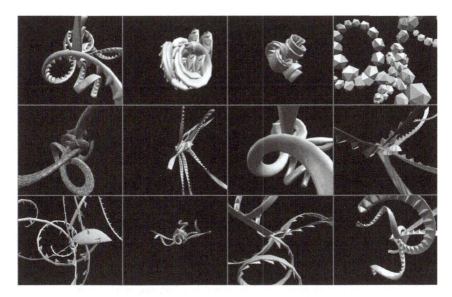

Figure 5.5 Twelve evolved forms from the interactive exhibit *Galápagos* by Karl Sims. The image in the upper left is the 'parent' and the other 11 images are its 'offspring' which have mutations in their genetic codes causing variations in their shape, texture and motion. Visit http://www.genarts. com/karl/ for more information (source: Image reproduced with permission. © 1997, Karl Sims, all rights reserved).

screens, each hosting an organism. The audience could exert pressure to 'shape the flow or random mutation' by standing on a pressure-sensitive pad in front of the preferred organism. The remaining 11 screens then showed the mutant offspring. Viewers could also choose more than one creature and breed their favourite combinations. According to some viewers, *Galápagos* was 'a potent demonstration that a dynamic interactive system can be as beautifully choreographed as a ballet' (Unger, 1999). This showed not only the power of Artificial Life as art but also as a means to study life itself. In fact, Sims experimented further to see whether evolution could take place without human intervention. Thus two at a time, his evolving virtual creatures were faced with a cube in an arena. The computer was to measure the creatures' success in gaining control over the cube. If they were successful, the creatures were allowed to mate. Mark Frauenfelder describes the result as follows:

> Over time – Sims has run some experiments out to 300 generations – the creatures started behaving like real animals, wanting nothing more than to seize and keep the cube. Some developed arms to reach out and encircle it; others evolved large flat bodies to cover it. Some walked toward the cube, others hopped, paddled, or crawled. Some developed

counterstrategies, learning to push opponents away form the object. One learned to grab the cube, then pin a smaller rival, preventing it from taking the cube back.

(1998)

Thus through this work it was possible to see how intelligent behaviour could evolve to survive an adverse environment. The interest in the piece's choreography produced by the abstract forms, striving to survive and progress, was akin to the aesthetic pleasure derived from watching life itself in its making and becoming in 'real' nature. In fact in Artificial Life it is the *becoming* of life, or, even better, the processes through which life changes, that are being watched.

Another well-known Artificial Life environment was Thomas Ray's *Tierra* (1991) (Figure 5.6), which presented a simulation of evolution in an attempt to study 'what happens when evolution by natural selection is embedded in the medium of digital computation' (Ray, 2003). In *Tierra* self-replicating machine code programmes evolved by natural selection and the system produced synthetic organisms which, by mutating, generated new forms. Here, as in nature, evolution proceeded by natural selection, without intervention

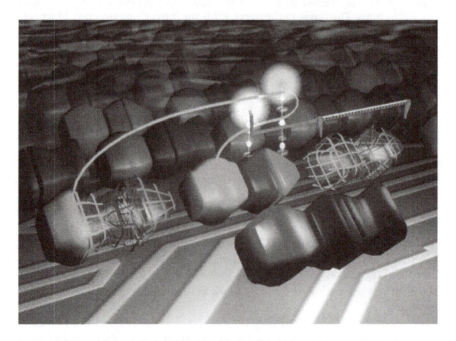

Figure 5.6 Tomas Ray, *Tierra*. A hyper-parasite (three-piece object below two spheres) steals the CPU from a parasite (left sphere). Using the stolen CPU and its own CPU (right sphere), it is able to produce two daughters (wire frame objects on left and right) simultaneously (source: Courtesy of Anti-Gravity Workshop).

by an operator. In fact, the different ecological communities that came of the system have been utilised to examine a number of ecological and evolutionary processes such as

> competitive exclusion and coexistence, host/parasite density dependant population regulation, the effects of parasites in enhancing community diversity, evolutionary arms race, punctuated equilibrium, and the role of chance and historical factors in evolution.
>
> (ibid.)

This may explain why some practitioners consider *Tierra* and similar programmes not as Artificial Life but as *life itself* (Hayles, 1999: 233, added emphasis).

Similar responses were produced by Steve Grand's *Creatures: An Exercise in Creation* (1997), which developed lifelike autonomous agents whose biology and biochemistry was described as being 'sufficiently complex as to be believable' (Kember, 2003: 91). As in Grand's words, each of the creatures in this computer game, called norns, is in fact

> composed of thousands of tiny simulated biological components, such as neurones, biochemicals, chemoreceptors, chemoemitters and genes. The norns' genes dictate how these components are assembled to make complete organisms, and the creatures' behaviour then emerges from the interactions of those parts, rather than being explicitly 'programmed in'.
>
> (2003)

The norns at one stage 'hovered around the five million mark', and, according to Grand, over one million people played the game. At one stage,

> there were something like four hundred websites run by Creatures enthusiasts, plus a highly active usenet newsgroup (alt.games.creatures). Specialised websites included adoption agencies for unwanted or battered norns (!), plus 'norn genome project' sites, where users try to unravel the meaning of the creatures' genome. All in all, Creatures became a vast, worldwide scientific experiment in artificial life.
>
> (ibid.)

The norns are able to learn about their environment, 'either by being shown things by their owners or through learning by their own mistakes' (ibid.). So, for instance, they learn how to find food, they can interact with their owners, form relationships and even produce offspring. They can also fall prey to a variety of diseases which can be treated with appropriate medicines. Most interestingly, although the viewer actually creates the norns, the viewer has no control over them. According to Sarah Kember,

> *Creatures* is by no means simply about interacting with virtual pets.
> Rather, the player is ultimately positioned as the observer of a process of
> evolution involving artificial life forms [with] which he or she has a
> degree of kinship. Norns are like children: a new generation.
>
> (2003: 97)

In the game the norns are 'free' to move and can be monitored through a
surveillance camera (ibid.). They are autonomous and independent from the
viewer. In other words, they constitute their own world. The popularity of
the game is unquestionably grounded in the 'principle that norns, as artificial life-forms are alive or possess the same essential life criteria as humans,
including autonomy, self-organisation and evolution' (ibid.).

In Artificial Life animals are not so much anomals as 'animats' (Wilson,
1991), i.e. artificial animals that exhibit learning behaviour by adapting to
their environment. Through them, it is possible not only to analyse human
and animal behaviour and evolution, but also to interact with it, to become
part of it. Via Artificial Life interactions, human beings are becoming
increasingly empowered to affect their own lives. Also, they are increasingly
able to watch their own evolution, their own becoming, as other. Not only
through the animat can information become alive, but the viewer can also
become a spectator of what is in all effects a game of life.

Christa Sommerer and Laurent Mignonneau

Experiments that have quite literally written the human presence within
Artificial Life environments have been conducted by the Austrian Christa
Sommerer and the Frenchman Laurent Mignonneau, who have been collabo-
rating since the early 1990s in creating interactive plant systems that allow
the viewer to act as the creator of the work of art. Since 1992, Sommerer and
Mignonneau have been working with 'natural interfaces' and created
'process-oriented art rather than pre-designed, predictable and object-
oriented art' (1999: 165). In fact, their works not only offer the viewer the
possibility of interaction and even creation of the work, but the artwork
itself is also often programmed to develop even after the end of the actual
interaction. In Sommerer and Mignonneau's interactive plant systems, the
work of art thus becomes an independent micro-ecological system, created
by the viewer and yet able to survive and evolve independently from them
(see Figure 5.7).

Their piece *Interactive Plant Growing* (1993) consisted of an interaction
between five real plants and five or more human viewers who could control
the growth of a number of artificial plants by touching the real plants. Here
the artists aimed at 'applying the Artificial Life principle to art projects'
(ibid.: 166) and thus creating artworks that were behaving like evolutionary
processes. In their subsequent piece *A-Volve* (1994), which was the result of
a collaboration with Ray, Sommerer and Mignonneau created an interactive

Figure 5.7 Interactive plant growing. © 1992, Christa Sommerer and Laurent Mignonneau. Interactive computer installation, collection of the Mediamuseum at the ZKM Karlsruhe.

computer installation which allowed the viewers to generate virtual three-dimensional creatures that lived in a water-filled glass pool. Here, viewers could design any kind of shape with their fingers on a touch screen and so 'give birth' to a number of artificial organisms (Sommerer and Mignonneau, 1998: 152) which could be interacted with through direct touch. As in the case of *Interactive Plant Growing*, the creatures were the product of evolutionary rules and could be influenced by human manipulation but also mate and produce offspring with their own genetic imprint. Not only, as in *Interactive Plant Growing*, was the virtual originated by the viewer but it was also able to 'outlive' the time of the interaction. In fact, the life of the virtual creature was dependent on the original interaction with the viewer but also the chance encounters with other members of its species which in turn had been created by other viewers at different points in time. 'The genetic work of art is no longer a static quantity; like nature itself, it is subject to constant non-linear mutations, changing itself and its observers' (Grau, 2003: 307).

In their subsequent piece, *Life Spacies* (1997), an evolutionary communication and interaction environment was created that allowed viewers to

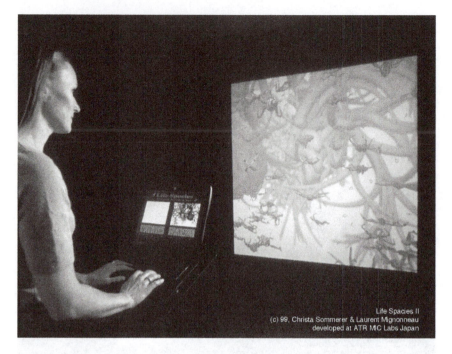

Figure 5.8 Life Spacies II. © 1997–9, Christa Sommerer and Laurent Mignonneau, collection of the NTT-ICC Museum Japan.

interact with each other remotely in a shared virtual environment (see Figure 5.8). Here, viewers could 'integrate themselves into a three-dimensional complex virtual world of artificial life organisms that react to their body movement, motion and gestures'. Moreover, online visitors could contribute to the installation from all over the world by sending an email message through the *Life Spacies* website. Each message initiated a creature and a corresponding sound: the more complex the message the more complex the creature. The creature's design could then evolve depending on the interaction with the viewers of the actual environment at the ICC-NTT Museum in Tokyo (Sommerer and Mignonneau, 1998: 157). Apart from the possibility of being born out of a viewer's design, these virtual creatures were able to 'clone' and thereby produce creatures with the same email text as the parent creature. They were also able to 'reproduce' and hence give life to creatures with an email text consisting of the original email texts of both parent creatures (Sommerer and Mignonneau, 2000).

Sommerer and Mignonneau's *Verbarium* (1999) was described as 'an inter-active text-to-form editor on the Internet'. Users here were able to write text messages which could function as a 'genetic code' for the creation of a visual three-dimensional form. As in Sommerer and Mignonneau's description, '[d]epending on the composition of the text, the form can either be simple or complex, or abstract or organic. All text messages together are used to build a collective and complex three-dimensional image' (in Weibel and Druckrey, 2001: 226). In *Verbarium*, not only did the organisms created by information provided by the viewers come to life but they were also capable of organising themselves into a 'superior' life form, a meta-text that was formed by and yet superseded the original individual text messages.

Langton claims that Artificial Life research does 'not only offer insight into life-as-we-know-it but can also afford a glimpse into life-as-it-could-be' (in Shanken, 1998: 383). While the anomal is becoming increasingly anomalous to us, animats are more and more significant to our understanding of what, at least theoretically, is possible with the 'becoming' of nature, culture and society. And so, while anomals are further and further removed from nature and society, animats are gradually becoming part of our everyday lives. In fact, whereas anomals are excluded from our domestic lives, animats are to be found in our houses, as our children's newest digital pets, or on our computers, an example of some of the latest distractions made available by technological innovation. And so curiously, whereas nature is becoming increasingly alien to us, Artificial Life offers the possibility of creating animals that are uncannily familiar to us. Thus the puppy lookalike AIBO ERS-111, developed by Sony Corporation (1999), makes more of a pet than Polly or OncoMouse®. Finally, through the anomal information becomes live, and through the animat, information *is* alive. It is this *liveness* of something that is ultimately non-organic, non-natural, not alive, though with Artificial Intelligence, that constitutes the most extra-ordinary aspect of the simulation of nature.

As Haraway suggests, genetic sciences and politics, and these, I believe, include A-Live practices, are at 'the heart of critical struggles for equality, democracy, and sustainable life' (1997: 62). Given that the commodification of what we commonly call nature is a clear sign of global power (Franklin *et al.*, 2000: 109), the possibility of a response to globalisation may lie in a 'revolution' of terms that sees, as in Alba's case, economic performance practices turned into artistic performance processes and Artificial Life performances offer models for biological life developments. Just as artistic performance can offer an insight into the mechanisms at the heart of commercial performance, Artificial Life could offer radical solutions not only to issues pertinent to nature and information, but also to politics and its role and impact on nature and society. Ultimately, of course, to deal with politics, is to deal with nature. As suggested by Bruno Latour, 'never, since the Greek's earliest discussions on the excellence of public life, have people spoken about politics without speaking of nature' since 'there has never been any other politics than the politics of nature, and there has never been any other nature than the nature of politics' (2004: 28).

6   Cell

Biological information is probably the most interesting information that we are deciphering and trying to decide to change. It's all a question of how – not if.

(Bill Gates in Stocker and Schöpf, 1999: 47)

Patenting Cell®™

The noun 'cell' stems from the Latin *cella*, indicating a storeroom, chamber or chapel (*OED*). The word is related to the Latin *celare*, to hide, to conceal, and derives from the Proto-Indo-European **kel*, which also produced the Old English word *hol*, cave, as well as the Gothic *halja*, Hell (ibid.). Moreover, a cell indicates a group of people working within a larger, often political or financial organisation. Having been described as the 'fundamental unit of our bodily communication network in the contemporary imagination', containing 'human life literally and symbolically' (Franklin *et al.*, 2000: 37), the cell functions both individually and as part of a whole. Yet there is something inherent in the etymology of the word that also indicates a process of concealment. While there is no question about a cell's actual existence, its capacity to act in 'disguise' may render it invisible, uncanny, even subversive.

The word 'corporation', which indicates 'the action of incorporating, the condition of being incorporated' (*OED*), derives from the Latin *corpus*, body. This suggests that there is a link between the biological body and the corporate body. Both rely on interconnectivity, depend on performativity, and have the capacity to re-present, re-brand, themselves in radical ways. Both, despite the fact that they appear as one, are constituted by a *multitude*. Because of their ability to disguise themselves, the cells that form the multitude may, however, not act in unison with the body. In other words, the cells' existence as a multitude does not imply their uniformity. Within the biological, financial and social spheres of the body, cells have the capacity to work in opposition. In fact, *cells are the smallest but also most crucially politically strategic units of biological, corporate and social bodies*.

The devastating power of individual cells is sadly known. From cancer to terrorism, the cell can bring destruction. However, the cell can also generate productive, and even profitable activity. So, for instance, cells can be used for repair work to cure cancers. Moreover, with the adoption of a technique that mimics the natural process of brain generation, laboratory-generated cells can help with Parkinson's, epilepsy and Alzheimer's. It is even possible to construct an 'assembly line for the manufacturing of unlimited quantities of human brain cells or neurons' (Connor, 2005). According to Bjorn Scheffler from the University of Florida: '[w]e can basically take these cells and freeze them until we need them. Then we thaw them, begin a cell generating process and produce a ton of new neurons' (in ibid.). As far as cellular productivity is concerned, it is not so much a matter of guarding oneself against a shortness of resources as of securing the ownership to cells in the first place.

Every cell of the body carries a complete copy of the genome. This means that each cell is a potentially endless source of information. But cells do not just perform in isolation, they also respond to their context. Interestingly, cells act on the information they receive from their neighbouring cells (Johnson, 2002: 86). Moreover,

> the extracellular matrix (ECM), once thought to be merely 'stuff between the cells' and a structural support for tissues, actually induces embryonic changes in tissues and plays a role in directing gene expression. Cellular interactions with ECM affect the way cells proliferate, adhere to surfaces, and migrate to other areas, which means that these signals affect the three-dimensional organisation and form of various tissues and organs. Without the right clues from other cells *and* from the material between cells, cells may not differentiate, perform specialised functions, or organise into larger structures. Thus the microarchitecture and spatial configurations of cells, as much as their cellular mechanisms, seem to be responsible for organ function.
>
> (Hogle in Franklin and Lock, 2003: 73–4)

In this way, each cell is not just individually responsible for its behaviour and function. Moreover, each cell depends on the in-between-cells. In other words, a cell's *environment* is just as responsible for its behaviour and function as its own content and architecture. In this sense, *a cell is a network*, storing, transmitting, receiving and elaborating information. What matters to this network is not just what actually constitutes it, but also what is outside of it, what is not actually part of it. *A cell is also not-a-cell.*

Increasingly, scientific research is aimed at cells, so much so that it is often said that the future of our species is inextricably tied to the outcomes of cell research. It is therefore not surprising that the market for the control of cells should have become one of the most lucrative, socially and politically strategic this millennium. James Thomson and John Gearhart's first culturing of stem cells in 1998 represents a key factor in this development.

Through the isolation of stem cells, which have the ability to produce all types of cells in the human body, it has become conceivable that a body would be able to re-generate, re-produce its failing parts. This understanding not only of body parts but also of actual cells as renewable commodities had vast social, philosophical, political and economic implications. Moreover, cells are not only valued as objects but also as information. Indeed, *the cell is priced according to the quality and accessibility of the information it contains*. Thus, for instance, molecular biologist and Nobel Laureate Walter Gilbert 'sees the essence of ourselves in terms of genetic information, predicting that soon one will be able to identify one's self by the information contained on a single compact disk (CD)' (in Kay, 2000: 327). It follows that not only will we be able, through cell-related technologies, to redesign and substitute our parts, but also the information that constitutes a specific human being, their intelligence, beauty, longevity, to name but a few, will herewith become transposable, patentable and even marketable.

Edward Yoxen pointed out that the reduction of life to the gene, and the gene to information, would lead to the 'capitalising' of life (1981: 112). This confirms that biological and corporate bodies are now, economically, inextricably linked. So, as Sarah Franklin notes, the human genome project could be seen as representing '*a molecular globalization of human kinship*' (2003, added emphasis). Thus while, on the one hand, the biotechnological revolution may constitute 'a morally necessary solution to the environmental and developmental crisis – to hunger, poverty and pollution problems, the conservation of biodiversity and climactic change' (Moser in Shiva and Moser 1995: 1), it also defines a radical development in world economics that will affect the way our society operates, and determine the need for new politics, philosophies and art practices. The birth of Dolly the sheep in 1996, which for many, as for Ian Wilmut, Dolly's creator, indicated the start of 'the age of biological control' (in Wilmut *et al.*, 2000: 17), in effect also signalled the beginning of a phase in the development of capitalism in which life itself can be translated into capital, or *Life*®™. Unsurprisingly, this process has led to an unprecedented intensification and multiplication of cellular, but also social and political control systems. From globalisation, and its homologising tendencies, to surveillance, monitoring us through our everyday life, to biopolitics, transforming humans, animals and plants into industrial systems whose success is determined by performativity, to cells, producing change from within, we are participating in the radical transformation of life in and around us into a controllable, purchasable and tradable commodity.

Franklin points out that '[t]he regenerative properties of cells [. . .] have become the objects of a major biotechnological futures market' (in Franklin and Lock, 2003: 97). Moreover, 'if human DNA sequences are to be the basis of future therapy, then the exclusive ownership of such DNA sequences would be money in the bank' (Lewontin in Bender and Druckrey, 1994: 119, added emphasis). While molecular biologists are turning into entrepreneurs, proposed changes in the patent laws are directed at 'actively encouraging (almost forcing) the commercialisation of inventions in both industrial and academic settings'. Meanwhile, 'the dovetailing of govern- mentally funded research with venture capital looking for investments' increasingly constitutes 'an expanded base for molecular biological research and development' (Rabinow, 1996: 19). As a consequence of the coming together of medical, political and economic concerns, possibly serious con- flicts of interest have begun to emerge in universities and in government ser- vices. Interestingly, some of these are caused by a loop in the law, which makes it impossible to patent 'natural things', but allows for the patenting of genes belonging to them, if presented in isolation. So, we learn, '*isolated genes are not natural* even though the organism from which they are taken may be'. This means that as whole beings, we are part of 'nature', but the multitude of cells that form us, if caught in isolation, is *un-natural*. It is clear that 'genomic biopower promises new levels of control over life through the pristine metalevel of "information", through control of the word, or the DNA sequence' (Kay, 2000: 327). This type of cellular control is entirely new in our society. Chris Hables Gray, for instance, narrates how a leukaemia sufferer found that UCLA had patented his genes and subse- quently licensed them to a number of corporations that were able, through the information contained in them, to produce a strong anticancer and antibacterial biochemical. Gray also notes how this episode revealed that whereas human beings cannot patent their own genes, corporations are able to do so (2001: 17). Without protection from the law, not only are we increasingly denaturalised, but our parts and even particles may in effect become someone else's 'private property'.

In 1980, the Supreme Court of the United States ruled by a vote of five to four that 'new life forms' fell under the jurisdiction of federal patent law. Following General Electric microbiologist Ananda Chakrabarty's develop- ment of a new bacterial strain capable of digesting a component of oil slicks with a clear utilitarian potential, the US Office of Technology Assessment commented: 'the question of whether or not an invention embraces living matter is irrelevant to the issue of patentability, as long as the invention is the result of human intervention' (in Rabinow 1996: 20). With respect to this growing tendency of transforming life into *Life*®™, Genewatch UK warned that 'genes exist in nature and cannot be considered to be "inven- tions"' and 'allowing the control of genetic information and how it is used to fall into private hands is dangerous' (2000: 3). Genewatch UK's fears, aimed particularly at Celera Genomics' attempt to gain a monopoly over all human genome data through what they perceive to be an 'aggressive patent- ing policy and refusal to lodge data with the public database, GenBank', of course, prompted British Prime Minister Tony Blair and US President Bill Clinton's calls for human genetic information to be 'freely available' (ibid.). Such calls, however, unless linked with effective legislation, have not as yet offered sufficient protection from the capitalisation of life implicit in the transformation of our cells into *Cells*®™.

According to Genewatch UK, evidence is 'emerging that patents on genes are actually hindering research in the public sector and creating monopolies on their use that will restrict their availability and may make medical products prohibitively expensive' (ibid.: 4). Genewatch UK argue that this will not only hold back public sector research but also act against competition in the private sector (ibid.: 5) and lead to the disturbing phenomenon of biopiracy in which 'available genetic resources are taken – very often from developing countries by companies or institutions of developed countries – and genes, cells or even whole organisms are patented and claimed as inventions' (ibid.). This worrying phenomenon, which has been described as a new form of 'genetic imperialism', is arising because companies from rich countries have started to claim patents on genes found in developing countries (ibid.: 3). Thus India, for instance, has been a special target of 'bioprospectors'. 'Relying on local knowledge of their medicinal and other properties, patents have been applied for on plants including turmeric, pepper and the neem tree, causing outrage among local growers' (ibid.: 6). This, of course, demonstrates that private companies are currently involved in large-scale sampling in the developed world in search for 'useful genes' that should have never left public property in the first place. DeCODE Genetics, for instance, has successfully negotiated with the Icelandic Government for 'exclusive access to the medical histories and tissue banks of all 270,000 Icelanders'. Hoffman-La Roche has subsequently 'agreed to pay up to $200 million for deCODE's Icelandic data on genetic causes of 12 common illnesses including diabetes and Alzheimer's disease' (ibid.: 7). More recently, Monsanto was awarded a patent for the wheat used for making chapati (Ramesh, 2004). These appropriations of life information for capital gain are increasingly creating a divide between the few who are able to amass biowealth and the multitude that, deprived of the right to own their own lives, are becoming trapped in a new form of bioslavery.

But this divide is not only between first and third world. Monsanto's own website, as noted by Graham Meikle, is an interesting example of the mixed economy of signals that the new phase of globalisation is able to create. The site presents the company as an environmentally friendly 'family' of workers:

> the company's 'family of 30,000 employees', who are committed to 'environmental sustainability'. An online slide show develops these themes of sustainability and family, beginning with images of the earth seen from space alongside text, which declares 'There's a family that lives here. A family that's lived here for thousands of years, getting to know the land and the oceans and the sky above'. *No mention is made of patenting them.*
>
> (2002: 129, added emphasis)

As suggested by Sir Walter Bodmer, Director of the Imperial Cancer Research Fund, as far as the human genome is concerned, 'the issue of ownership is at the heart of everything we do' (in Bender and Druckrey, 1994: 120). And since there is no question that the '*human genome must be freely available to all humankind*' (Genewatch UK, 2000: 7, original emphasis), and that the populace should have the right to the cells, genes and proteins that constitute its own medicines, produce and even body parts, a new form of biopolitics and regulatory bio-legislation needs to be introduced before the majority of the world population will be deprived of the very cells that *are* them. It is unquestionable that without that demo-cracy will come to an end.

Semi-living art: Eduardo Kac, Marcel-lì Antúnez Roca, Oron Catts, Ionat Zurr and SymbioticA

Developments in scientific and technological research have inspired a number of artists to engage with the production of life. Among these is Eduardo Kac, who, in the transgenic artwork *Genesis* (1998–2004) (see Figure 6.1), claims to have explored 'the intricate relationship between biology, belief systems, information technology, dialogical interaction, ethics and the Internet' (in Ascott, 2000: 17). For *Genesis* Kac encoded a passage from the Bible that stated: '[l]et man have dominion over the fish of the sea and over the fowl of the air and over every living thing that moves upon the earth'. Through a conversion principle by which a dash became T (Thiamine), a dot became C (Cytosine), a word space became A (Adenine), and a letter space became G (Guanine), Kac was able

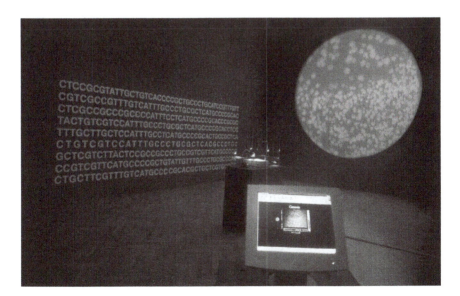

Figure 6.1 Eduardo Kac, *Genesis*, 1999. Transgenic net installation (detail) (source: Courtesy of Eduardo Kac).

to 'translate' the passage into a synthetic 'art gene' (Tomasula in Kostic and Dobrila, 2000: 86). This could mutate as remote participants activated a source of ultraviolet light in the gallery through the Internet, thus changing the original meaning of the biblical text (Stocker in Kostic and Dobrila, 2000: 82). In Steve Tomasula's words, sequences like AGC | GCT | ACC formed particular amino acids and each DNA molecule then became 'both material and message, both the book and its content' (Tomasula in Kostic and Dobrila, 2000: 86). In this sense, *Genesis* is characteristic of a number of bioart works. It is non-evolutionary, devoid of purpose, *alive*, and performative in nature. It treats information not only as content but also as a material that quite literally shapes the work. Thus in *Genesis*, information *becomes* life. The piece is more about creation, as the title suggests, than about the evolution of life itself, which exists almost as a byproduct of the event. In fact, life in *Genesis* appears to have no use or function, except at the level of communication. Life = information = art = information = life, and so on.

Opposite dynamics were present in Marcel-lì Antúnez Roca's *Epiphany* (1999), which was described as 'a space for in-depth reflection on the relationships between human beings and the worlds of biology (bacterias) [*sic*], technology (prosthesis, interactivity), culture (languages) and mythology (fiction and fantasy)' (Anon, 2002). The work consists of four installations: 'Agar' (see Figure 6.2), 'Requiem', 'Alphabet' and 'Caprice'. In 'Agar', there were two Winogradsky columns containing anaerobic bacteria, some Petri

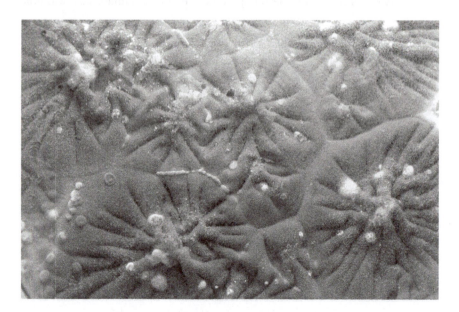

Figure 6.2 'Agar', Marcel-lí Antúnez Roca. Fungus detail. Marcel.lí Antúnez Roca + Ph: Darius Koehli (source: Courtesy of Marcel.lí Antúnez Roca).

dishes containing agar nutrients for fungi and a display with a fish tank for the cyanobacteria (Giannetti, 1999: 104). Unlike in Kac's *Genesis*, what mattered here, was the actual process of evolution seen as the 'transformation undergone by different bacteria and fungi cultures' (ibid.). In fact, as Claudia Giannetti notes, '[t]he Petri dishes [. . .] and their life cycle provide a perfect example of this polarity between evolution and devolution, between dominant and dominated beings, between adaptability and inadaptability, between mortality and immortality' (ibid.: 192). Thus the significance of 'Agar' 'does not lie in the solid objects of which it is composed, but in the ephemeral communities of micro-organisms which grow, reproduce and die' (ibid.: 104). In this work, it is clear that as soon as the evolution and devolution of cells, proteins and bacteria are at stake, the whole issue of control becomes of paramount importance.

Similar complexity is present in the biotechnological experimentation of the laboratory SymbioticA. Established in 2000 and located in the School of Anatomy and Human Biology at the University of Western Australia, SymbioticA, acts 'as a porous membrane in which art and bio-medical sciences and technologies could mingle'. Claiming to be the first laboratory of its kind that 'enables artists to engage in wet biology practices in a biological science department', SymbioticA sees its strength in its 'non-scientific approach to science'. The laboratory, which declares itself to be inspired by art, rather than by scientific experimentation or economic reasoning, has been successfully developing, among a variety of projects, what it has itself named 'semi-living' art objects (SymbioticA, 2005).

For *Tissue Culture and Art Project* (TC&A), initiated in 1996, and in many ways a precursor to SymbioticA, Oron Catts and Ionat Zurr have been cultivating tissue cultures through tissue engineering 'as a medium for artistic expression'. To them, their creations are 'animate *and* inanimate, both part of an organism *and* outside of it'. Catts and Zurr, who argue that new technologies such as the ones adopted in their work will have a 'dramatic effect on human evolution and human history in the near future' aimed at the creation of 'designed biological objects', or 'semi-living objects (products)', devoid of medical or agricultural value or purpose. Here, 'new and functional living tissue is fabricated using living cells, which are usually associated in one way or another with a matrix or scaffolding to guide tissue development' (Catts and Zurr, 2002: 365, added emphasis). Tissue cells were harvested through biopsy either from living animal bodies, those butchered for food, or bodies that were sacrificed for the experiment. Animals used in this manner included rabbits, rats, mice and humans. Connective tissue from mice, rats and pigs, muscle tissue from rats, sheep and goldfish, bone and cartilage tissues from pigs, rats, humans and sheep, bone marrow stem cells from pigs and neurons from goldfish were also used (Thacker, 2005: 367). The cells were then seeded on a coated petri-dish tissue culture flask, or three-dimensional polymer and hydrogel constructs where the tissue was kept alive in an attempt 'to emulate their original environment'. Furthermore, ethical consideration, which clearly arose out of the fact that the sculptures were alive, prompted reflections about the works' conservation and care (ibid.: 366). Thus, the cells' environments had to satisfy a series of requirements that were subject to rigid controls: nutrients and other biological agents had to be supplied, waste was removed, and homeostasis (including temperature, pH levels, dissolved gas levels) was maintained, while the content of the bioreactor was kept sterile (ibid.: 367). The cells hence became 'partial life forms', constituted by 'a part of a complex living being sustained outside and independent from the body' (Catts in Heathfield, 2003: 153). In this sense the semi-living statue is never just formed by the cells that constitute the work, but also by their actual environment.

In *Tissue Culture and Art(ificial) Womb* (2000), TC&A grew what has been described as 'modern versions of the legendary Guatemalian worry dolls in the artificial womb' (ibid.: 368) (see Figure 6.3). These 'were hand crafted out of degradable polymers (PGA and P4HB) and surgical sutures, 'sterilized and seeded with endothelial, muscle, and obsteoblasts cells ([. . .] bone tissue) that are grown over/into the polymers'. The polymers degraded while the tissue grew, and so the sculptures acquired their own structure and shape. As a result, Catts notes, 'the dolls become partially alive.' These combinations of 'object and a being' are genderless, new 'art breeds', 'both grown and born', at the same time natural and un-natural. Made of 'both synthetic materials and living biological matter from complex organisms', they 'blur the boundaries between what is born/manufactured, animate/ inanimate.' Here, human-made and natural materials coexists symbiotically and originally, biologically and aesthetically. As in the case of Kac's *Genesis*, the works have no agricultural or medical accountability – they just *are*, in *excess* of evolution. Occupying an 'ambiguous intermediary zone between subject and object, a sort of "tissue actant", more than an inert object and less than an autonomous organism (Thacker, 2005: 309), the worry dolls, and semi-living art in general, surpass the ontological sophistication of the cyborg and signal that art's response to the capitalisation of life operates at the level of *surplus*.

Catts and Zurr have also been in dialogue with Stelarc who, in his *Extra Ear* project (1997–) has been looking at the possibility of constructing a third ear that could be positioned next to his real ear to 'speak to anyone who would get close to it' and perhaps 'whisper sweet nothings to the other ear'. Considering the ear as the organ of balance (Stelarc, 2002), Stelarc claims that the creation of an extra ear would unbalance both the relationship between the viewer and the work of art and the relationship between the human and the world of information technology. As in Stelarc's words, '[t]hese performances are about technology viewed as a symptom of excess rather than a sign of lack' (ibid.). Thus through TC&A, *Extra Ear $\frac{1}{4}$ Scale* (2003–) was developed using human cells as a $\frac{1}{4}$ scale replica of Stelarc's own ear (Figure 6.4). Stelarc notes:

Figure 6.3 'A Semi-Living Worry Doll, H.'. Artists: The Tissue Culture & Art Medium McCoy Cell line, biodegradable/bioabsorbable polymers and surgical sutures. Dimension of original: $2\,cm \times 1.5\,cm \times 1\,cm$. Date: from The Tissue Culture & Art(ificial) Wombs Installation, Ars Electronica 2000 (source: Courtesy of Oron Catts and Ionat Zurr).

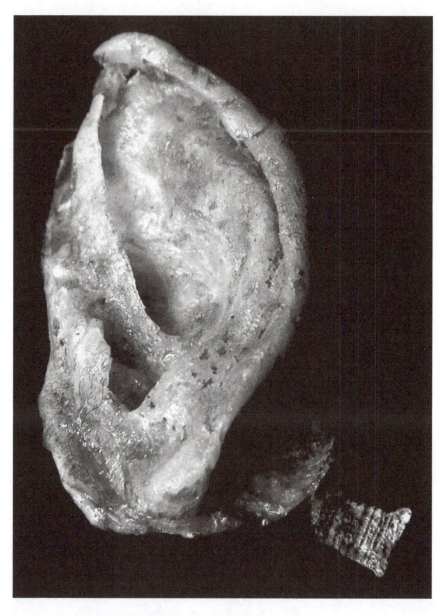

Figure 6.4 EXTRA EAR ¼ SCALE, Galerija Kapelica, Ljubljana, 13–20 May 2003
(source: Photographer: Ionat Zurr. Stelarc with TC&A).

[t]he ear is cultured in a rotating micro-gravity bioreactor which allows the cells to grow in a 3D structure. The ear will be fed with nutrients every 3–4 days in a sterile hood. Once the ear can be grown with my own bone marrow cells it would be possible to insert it beneath the skin of the forearm as a first step to construct an ear on the arm. The skin of the forearm is smooth and would adequately stretch without the necessity of any inflating prosthesis. The ear on the arm could be constructed with less complex surgical intervention. And disconnected from the face, the ear on the arm could be guided and pointed in different directions.

(Stelarc, 2005)

Figure 6.5 EAR-ON-ARM VISUALIZATION, Melbourne, 2003 (source: Photographer: Polixeni Papapetrou. STELARC).

The piece, Stelarc and TC&A claim, is about two 'collaborative concerns'. First, the ear constitutes 'a recognizable human part and is meant to be ulti-mately attached to the body as a soft prosthesis. However it is being pre-sented as partial life and brings into question the notions of the wholeness of the body.' Stelarc also notes that the piece is aimed at confronting 'society's cultural perceptions of life with the increasing ability to manipulate living systems [. . .] The prosthesis is now a partial life form – partly constructed and partly alive' (ibid.). *Extra Ear $\frac{1}{4}$ Scale* utilises human-made *alive* prosthetics which augment the body through real flesh, grown externally, un-naturally, anomalously from Stelarc. Stelarc, however, is equally *present* in his own body and in the cells that are grown *outside* of him, in *excess* of him, and which are to be returned to him, for his own (medically, economically, politically) 'unneces-sary' *augmentation.* Apart from drawing attention to the fact that the post-human body is always already dispersed, a network of possibilities, this smaller ear, precisely because of its 'uselessness', its 'unnaturalness', constitutes a 'bioart-object' whose 'performance' is not determined by functionality, not even in terms of the body it originates from, or longs to go back to, but rather aesthetics. In other words, the semi-living sculpture, precisely because its surplus of liveness, its dis-functionality, and in-valuable anomaly, resists commodification, and so by default, falls into the realm of art.

Tissue engineering, and subsequently biologically inspired bioart, were the result of the biomedical exploration of the possibility of creating spare body parts. Catts notes that 'the body is now seen as a regenerative entity that can be healed using its own parts (cells, tissues), which are taken outside of it, treated, manipulated and re-implanted back into the body'. Because of this, 'parts of complex organisms are designed and grown independently of the organism from which it is originally derived'. 'Constituting a challenge to the Western concepts of self, body, life and death' (in Heathfield, 2003: 155), these bioartworks revolutionalise our understanding of what an art object can be, aesthetically and ontologically, but also ethically, politically and philo-sophically. Unquestionably, semi-living bio-objects are to become a growing and crucial part of our everyday life. And so we too, of course, in the process of becoming post-human, will also become 'semi-living': part human, part animal, part machine, and possibly also part object.

The cellular practice of the Critical Art Ensemble

There is a clear connection between the processes at the heart of globalisa-tion and the biotechnological industry's transformation of life into the global product *Life*®™. Already Michel Foucault had shown that '[t]he control of society over individuals is not conducted only through conscious-ness or ideology, but also in the body and with the body' (in Hardt and Negri, 2000: 27). This suggests that in today's capitalist society the highest form of control is in fact not external, but internal to the body. Subse-quently, biopolitics, the politics that controls 'the biological, the somatic, the corporeal' (ibid.), indicating the programme 'of direct political and cultural intervention in the body' (György in Heller and Puntscher Riekmann, 1996: 41), is not only the principal motor of globalisation but also the starting point of a possible response to it.

As shown by Hardt and Negri, biopower is a form of power in which what is at stake 'is the production and reproduction of life itself' (2000: 24). In other words, biopower, to facilitate the production and propagation of globalisation, regulates life. Because of this, as Negri suggests, biopower cannot but lead to a homogenisation of the population, which is already becoming, in his words, 'an ensemble of coexisting living beings who present particular onto-biological characteristics and whose life is susceptible to being controlled in order to ensure, with a better management of the labour-force, an ordered growth of society' (2003: 79). Globalisation means that the globe, its cities and lands, plants and animals, humans and cells, are being turned into a system of production. At this stage in the development of capitalism, biopower has penetrated all spheres of life and a response to globalisation must begin at the level of an ethical form of biopolitics. To be effective, this new form of political practice must be at once global and cellular.

One of the groups which has most originally and successfully pursued this objective through theatre is the North American collective, Critical Art Ensemble whose texts have been translated in at least eight languages and whose art has been seen internationally, both in 'real' and in virtual locations. Through their publications, web activity and performance, Critical Art Ensemble works to denounce the dangerous links between globalisation and the biotechnological industries. This is evident at a number of levels. First, their work is rhizomatic, non-locable, 'global'. This non-locability, or inter-locability is also evident in its interdisciplinary breadth. The company in fact works at the point of intersection between art, technology, critical theory and political activism. Notably, the word intersection here is crucial, since the work literally resides between these different, but interrelated areas. According to the Ensemble,

> one local group cannot depend on intersubjective experience as a means to acquire political support for their cause. Globalization has created a new theatre that bursts the boundaries of the theatre of everyday life. We now have a theatre of activism that has emerged out of the necessity of taking material life struggles into hyperreality.
>
> (Critical Art Ensemble, 1996: 94)

The theatre of Critical Art Ensemble thus operates through sets of inter-related interventions, which take place in the everyday as well as in virtual reality. Through this plurality of interventions, Critical Art Ensemble is able to utilise the mechanisms of globalisation and expose them from within. Thus the company's curiously hyperreal theatre allows for a dialogue between politics, art, new media and critical theory, which is able to challenge preconceptions about the relationship between globalisation, science and art precisely because of its ability to dislocate and 'burst' its disciplinary and aesthetic boundaries.

There are a number of features that render this work particularly important within the fields of radical, political, but also post-modern, and new media theatre. These are its capacity to combine different and even seemingly contrasting media and discourses; its ability to perform 'invisibly' and to address wide, 'global', audiences; and its interest in blurring science and art, technology and theatre, post-modernism and politics. Another salient feature of its work is its dispersal. Though determinant in challenging social preconceptions, their actions tend to be invisible, 'rhizomatic'. The company have in fact recognised that 'power in pancapitalism has become nomadic, decentered (or at least multicentered), and global' (in Schneider, 2000: 125). So, to propose a form of theatre and/or activism that critiques globalisation, a multifocal and decentered response is fundamental, since direct political intervention necessitates 'invisibility and non-locatability' (ibid.: 131).

Founded in 1987, Critical Art Ensemble works both electronically and in 'real' locations. The electronic actions are a fundamental part of its work since members argue that '[f]or information economies, the net is the apparatus of command and control' and so invariably '[t]he net is culturally and politically bordered' (Critical Art Ensemble, 1995). For them, it is important to act as a destabilising and critical presence online. For this purpose, the company has been utilising electronic civil disobedience (ECD) as an 'option for digital resistance' (Critical Art Ensemble, 1996: 13) since 1994. To the Ensemble, ECD represents 'an inversion of the model of civil disobedience'. Thus, rather than aspire to a mass movement of public objectors, ECD aims towards a 'flow of particularized micro-organizations (*cells*) that would produce multiple currents and trajectories to slow the velocity of capitalist political economy' (ibid.: 14, added emphasis). The company is among the principal theorists and activists of ECD, through which it has been offering a continuous and corroding critique of capitalist production processes while also creating an efficacious post-Brechtian model of post-modern political activism. By working both politically and aesthetically on the fringes, Critical Art Ensemble has thus been able to present one of the most complex models for civil practice (and 'disobedience') to date. Whether this work is first encountered online, or live, in a university, a street or a gallery, at its heart is the simple and yet overwhelmingly powerful idea that theatre, whether 'real' or virtual, can at least temporarily displace its audience. It is this dis-location, this *Verfremdung* that allows for a cutting insight into the 'globalised' world of the biotechnology industries.

The company defines its practice as a 'recombinant theatre' formed by 'interwoven performative environments through which participants may flow' (ibid.: 87). I have already introduced the company's digital, online activity. The other main environment utilised is constituted by the 'theatre of everyday life', which includes street theatre, as well as happenings, and other non-matrixed forms, achieved through 'ephemeral, autonomous situations from which temporary public relationships emerge that can make possible critical dialogue on a given issue' (ibid.). The company's performative environments are participatory and it is in the actual interaction with the audience, that the aesthetics and politics of its work operate at their most complex levels. Interestingly, the company perceives a marked difference between pedagogical and political actions. According to its members, pedagogical actions can in fact 'slide into the space between location and dislocation, visibility and invisibility', whereas political actions necessitate 'invisibility and non-locatability' (in Schneider, 2000: 126). Thus the participatory events, through their non-matrixed, intangible, uncanonic nature, maintain primarily a pedagogical role while their online, virtual existence is more directly political precisely because of its cellular invisibility and non-locatability. Critical Art Ensemble argues that under the capitalist regime, individuals will be 'forced to submit their bodies for reconfiguration so they can function more efficiently under the obsessively rational imperatives of pancapitalism'. According to CAE, the body of the future will be 'a solid entity whose behaviours are fortified by task-oriented technological armor interfacing with ideologically engineered flesh' (Critical Art Ensemble, 2003). Already, the Ensemble claims, soldiers are no longer soldiers but 'weapon systems' (Critical Art Ensemble, 1998: 27). Thus for them, the 'biological body, or more precisely, the privatisation, manipulation, and commodification of the *organic*, is the "new frontier" that capital is "penetrating"' (Schneider, 2000: 128).

The collective sees science as the new religion, 'the institution of authority regarding the production of knowledge', which defines concepts and practices such as nature in terms of 'the political economy of the day' and also represents 'a key mediator of the public's relationship with nature' (Critical Art Ensemble, 1996: 40). CAE thus argues that assisted genetic reproduction can function as a form of eugenics adopted in order 'to give that child a predisposition for a competitive edge in the open market (higher intelligence, better health, better dexterity, more desirable appearance, etc.)'. According to CAE, '[t]he values/needs of capital are now being inscribed on the body at a molecular level' (ibid.: 54). To counteract this, Critical Art Ensemble works at the level of 'cellular practice' (ibid.: 69), with a digital aesthetics functioning by copying, which represents 'a process that offers dominant culture minimal material for recuperation by recycling the same images, actions, and sounds into radical discourse' (ibid.: 77). This copy-cut-paste technique is visible not only in the deliberate recycling of ideas between the live and virtual actions, as well as between the company's own critical theory, available on its website, and its practice, but also in the carefully constructed collages of facts and fiction, real and simulated, theatre and lecture, that constitute its performance events. And it is precisely within this ability to work at a rhizomatic, cellular level that the company's most original and politically effective reply to empire is located. In fact, through its cellular activity, Critical Art Ensemble is able to show us how to rewrite the production systems that propel globalisation from within.

The main aims of this interdisciplinary hyperreal theatre are the demystification of transgenic production, the addressing of public fear in relation to it, the promotion of critical thinking/art, the opening of the halls of science to public scrutiny and, ultimately but also very importantly, 'the dissolution of the cultural boundaries of specialisation' (Critical Art Ensemble, 2002: 59). Unsurprisingly, its works are structured deceptively so that what are clearly carefully put together theatrical performances are presented as seemingly spontaneous interactions around information points where fliers, pamphlets and computer monitors can be freely consulted by the general public. Standing nearby to the displays, the collective presents itself as a company *performing* a particular mission. By creating a kind of invisible theatre, Critical Art Ensemble, which quotes as its models the Living Theatre, the Theatre of the Oppressed, Guerrilla Art Action Group, Rebel Chicano Art Front and the Situationists (Critical Art Ensemble, 1996: 87), is thus able to approach its unaware audience on subjects of ultimate controversy.

For instance, in the performance of *Flesh Machine* (1997–8) Ensemble members introduced themselves as BioCom, a company whose mission is 'Building a better organic platform' for the planet (see Figure 6.6). Here, they *performed* as a business aiming to assist 'in the reconfiguration of the body to help it to adjust to the intensified rigors of pancapitalist imperatives and to adopt to its pathological environment'. Claiming maintenance over 'the largest sperm and egg bank in the market', as well as the ownership of a large pharmaceutical company aiming at the medicinal, the recreational and the spiritual, the company thus portrayed itself as a 'leader in the emerging field of genomics', able to advise about a more efficient way of using reproduction so that

> no useless activity occurs in the reproductive process, and less genetic material is wasted. Excess genetic material is reconfigured into a substance for commodified process [. . .] Let BioCom demonstrate that a 'better baby' (one better adapted to the imperatives of pancapitalism) can be produced through rationalized intervention.
>
> (Critical Art Ensemble, 2004)

But BioCom is not only seen to rid the human species of terrible diseases, but also to promote the 'rational' redesign and engineering of 'body functions and psychological characteristics that refuse ideological inscription' (ibid.). The piece, highlighting the links between reproductive technologies and eugenics, even featured genetic screening of its audience members as well as the presentation of the diary of a couple going through assisted reproduction. Here the physiological and the political merged and the body quite literally became the site for biopolitics.

Another performance piece, *Society for Reproductive Anachronisms*

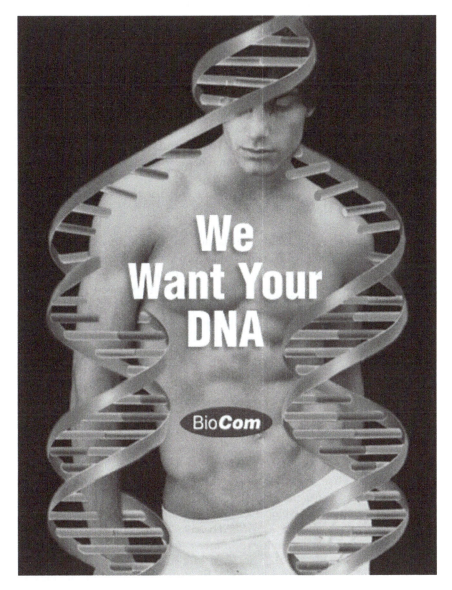

Figure 6.6 Critical Art Ensemble, *Flesh Machine*. Poster (source: Courtesy of Critical
Art Ensemble).

(1999–2000), follows similar but diametrically opposite dynamics in that,
on this occasion, information on genetic experimentation in reproductive
technologies was presented by the company as if it comprised a group of
'activists who spoke to people about the dangers of medical intervention in
the reproductive process'. Here, Critical Art Ensemble introduced itself as a

society formed in 1992 'to combat the rationalization and instrumentaliza-
tion of the reproductive process that is occurring in order to totally manage
its service to the pancapitalist order'. Thus the collective's aims were said to
be, among others, the resistance to eugenics, the maintenance of the connection between sexuality and reproduction, the disruption of the commodification of flesh, the exposure of the politics of reproductive technology, and the
disturbance of 'the waters of capital's gene pool'. After an 'informative'
section, the company presented a 'know your genetic future' questionnaire
in which the viewers could find out whether they were 'a flesh market reject,
or booty for the DNA pirates' (Critical Art Ensemble, 2004a).

When performing the piece at Rutgers University, Critical Art Ensemble
also drew the viewers' attention to sperm and egg donor recruitment on university campuses in North America for use in what they claim to be 'neo-
eugenic practices'. Here it created

> the illusion that a reprotech company visiting Rutgers was actively
> recruiting a sperm donor for a woman who was monitoring the process
> online from Florida. (In actuality, the performer was in a back room in
> the building, but it read perfectly as a transborder process.) The effective-
> ness of this technology was due to the looping back of the virtual into
> real space, and a surrendering of interactivity in favor of participation.
>
> (Critical Art Ensemble, 1996: 97)

As in other pieces, it was the deliberate blurring of facts and fiction that left
this audience uncertain, not only about what was real and what was simulated, but also about the uncanny relationship between the science of
theatre, and its obsession with truthfulness and representation, and the
theatre of science, and its disturbing ability to re-create life.

In its most recent performance piece, *GenTerra* (2001–3), Critical Art
Ensemble introduced itself as a company adopting 'transgenic solutions for a
greener world'. Here it claimed to be aiming to 'discover and create products for resource management that are harmonious with the ecosystem in
which they function'; 'develop biological environmental resource management initiatives that serve as an alternative to chemical environmental
resource management'; 'refine techniques of biological environmental
resource management, so that its past disasters will not be repeated';
and 'explore the options offered by new breakthroughs in biotechnology so
that they may be used as a resource that functions in the public interest'.
As *GenTerra*, Critical Art Ensemble claims to be presenting both 'the good
and bad news' regarding the possibility of a transgenic ecology so that
'people can make up their own minds about these extremely complex issues'
(Critical Art Ensemble, 2004b).

I saw the piece at the Natural History Museum in London in the summer
of 2003. Typically, the company had created a display with a number of
computers that the audience could consult in order to learn about the work

Figure 6.7 Critical Art Ensemble, *GenTerra*, bacteria release machine (source: Courtesy of Critical Art Ensemble).

of GenTerra and similar companies. Again, facts and fiction were carefully interwoven so that it was difficult to tell them apart. Without hiding the performative nature of their event (a large poster introducing the piece as 'theatre' – 'Critical Art Ensemble presents GenTerra' – was displayed near the tables), the performers, wearing white medical gowns and appropriate nametags, approached the audience to discuss GenTerra's mission and performance. Surrounded by other displays presenting 'real' scientific projects and in the presence of 'real' scientists, swiftly crossing Darwin Centre's busy corridors, the performance of *GenTerra* tended to disappear against the museum's flow of everyday life. As in other pieces, the interaction with the audience led to an actual experiment. A number of volunteers gave blood for the making of some of the bacteria in advance of the event. During the performance, participants to the project would then decide whether or not to activate the 'transgenic bacteria release machine' (ibid.) that allowed them to prepare samples for their own use and so be able to walk off GenTerra's display centre with a sample of recombinant bacteria containing a complete random human genome library. Although I quite deliberately set off that day to see Critical Art Ensemble at work, I was uncertain as to what was happening in front of my eyes. Was it all 'real'? Or was it theatre? Not only was I mostly unable to decode fact from fiction, but also, more worryingly, I was unsure as to what the transgenic bacteria release machine actually was. Could it *really* generate bacteria? Were there any there? Were we safe?

Figure 6.8 Critical Art Ensemble, *GenTerra*. Screen shot of GenTerraCD ROM (source: Courtesy of Critical Art Ensemble).

This 'confusion' is of course part of Critical Art Ensemble's mission. For CAE, '[c]onfusion should be seen as an acceptable aesthetic. The moment of confusion is the pre-condition for the scepticism necessary for radical thought to emerge' (in Meikle, 2002: 132). So what *really* happened? First of all, the transgenic bacteria release machine could not really generate bacteria. The machine simply consisted of ten sample dishes, nine of which had wild bacteria or moulds collected from the area while the tenth contained recombinant bacteria. The characters in the piece and their affiliations, as in all their works, were fictional and yet the scientific information provided and the processes presented were truthful. The piece in itself was an act of theatre, though most of the documentation presented was factually correct. And yet, despite its *visibility*, this cellular practice became *invisible*. The fiction, however manifest, disappeared. The signifiers flickered. This spectator was allowed to become doubtful.

Through its work, Critical Art Ensemble not only exploits and simultaneously denounces the *performance* of globalisation but it also draws our attention to the plurality of ways in which corporate capitalism, and thus empire, is rewriting life itself. By *acting* this out in all the levels of its work, Critical Art Ensemble is able to operate rhizomatically, thus effectively challenging globalisation from within by utilising its very own languages and communication systems. And yet it is precisely by exposing these mechanisms through theatre that the company allows for the possibility of change. Not only does it create a platform through which to educate audiences who, like me, find it difficult to extricate scientific and economic fact from fiction within the fast-changing field of biotechnology, but it also effectively presents itself as a model of actual change, indicating how it is possible to work within the industry without subscribing to its capitalist processes.

However, shortly after the London performance the company's aesthetic of confusion was profoundly misinterpreted. On 11 June 2004, Steve Kurtz, a founding member of Critical Art Ensemble, and also Associate Professor of Art at the University of Buffalo, awoke to find that Hope Kurtz, his wife of over 20 years had unexpectedly died. Subsequent investigations found the cause of death to be a fatal heart attack. However, the paramedics at the scene had become alarmed at the scientific materials in Kurtz's house and called the FBI and the Joint Terrorism Task Force. The property was then cordoned off, Hope Kurtz's body, the couple's computer, books and papers seized and Steve Kurtz arrested. It emerged that, under the Patriot Act, it is now illegal in the United States to use biological research material and that

> Whoever knowingly possesses any biological agent, toxin, or delivery system of a type or in a quantity that, under the circumstances, is not reasonably justified by a prophylactic, protective, bona fide research, or other peaceful purpose, shall be fined under this title, imprisoned not more than ten years or both.

Kurtz, in collaboration with Beatriz da Costa, was in fact utilising some harmless bacteria for the performance/exhibition, *The Interventionists*, due to be held at the Massachusetts Museum of Contemporary Art. In the piece the company aimed at determining whether certain foods contained genetically modified organisms and thus raise awareness about genetically modified food.

Shortly after Kurtz's arrest, subpoenas were issued to a number of people working with him: Adele Henderson, Chair of the Art Department at the University of Buffalo; Andrew Johnson, Professor of Art at Buffalo and member of Critical Art Ensemble; Paul Venouse, Professor of Art at Buffalo; Beatriz da Costa, Professor of Art at the University of California at Irvine and member of Critical Art Ensemble; Steven Barnes, Florida State University and Critical Art Ensemble member; and Dorian Burr and Beverly Shlee, also members of the collective. A Grand Jury was subsequently convened at the behest of the FBI with the apparent intent of collecting evidence to indict Kurtz on charges of possessing biological materials though Kurtz and his colleague, Dr Robert Ferrell, Professor of Genetics at the University of Pittsburgh, who had allegedly helped him to procure the bacteria, were finally arraigned on charges of mail and wire fraud which carry a maximum sentence of 20 years in prison. Under the arraignment conditions, Kurtz was subject to travel restrictions, random and scheduled visits by a probation officer and periodic drugs tests. Following his arrest, and a defense campaign mounted by ®TMark, which left some wondering about the truthfulness of the story, letters and petitions were circulated and signed by scholars from a variety of fields. Many individuals also signed – including industrialists, biologists, microbiologists, epidemiologists, environmentalists, lawyers and attorneys. Interestingly, signatures came not only from the United States but also from Europe, New Zealand, South America, Taiwan, Australia, Iceland, South Africa, Singapore, Canada, South Korea, India and Japan. One of the petitions, signed by some 36 US West Coast academics – the top researchers in the field of new media at the Universities of Santa Barbara, Berkeley, Irvine and San Diego – sums up the general concern:

> we see here a pattern of behaviour that leads to the curtailing of academic freedom, freedom of artistic expression, freedom of interdisciplinary investigation, freedom of information, exchange, freedom of knowledge, accumulation and reflection, and freedom of bona fide and peaceful research. All of which are fundamental rights and cornerstones of a modern academic environment.
>
> (in Critical Art Ensemble, 2004c)

If the Patriot Act allows for the use of the agents in 'prophylactic, protective, bona fide research, or other peaceful purpose' why was Kurtz's artistic work, which was carried out openly, primarily in museums, but also at universities and in a whole variety of performance spaces, with the aim to educate and distribute knowledge, framed as bioterrorism? Is theatre no longer considered 'bona fide' or 'peaceful'? How could there have been such 'confusion'? How could props be mistaken for biological weapons and an artist for a terrorist?

As suggested by the journal *Nature*: '[a]s with the persecution of some scientists in recent years, it seems that government lawyers are singling Kurtz out as a warning to the broader artistic community' (Editorial, 2004: 685). But a warning for what? Clearly the work of the Critical Art Ensemble is peaceful and educational. As in the words of D.A. Henderson, M.D., M.P.H., Senior Advisor of the Center for Biosecurity of the University of Pittsburgh Medical Center:

> I am absolutely astonished [. . .] based on what I have read and understand, Professor Kurtz has been working with totally innocuous organisms. [. . .] I am dismayed by what appears to me to be yet one more instance in which knowledgeable persons in the field of bioterrorism are not being brought in and consulted to ascertain what might be real problems and what are purely spurious problems.
>
> (ibid.)

This proves, if anything, how necessary and successful the work of the Critical Art Ensemble has been and still is, and how crucial it is, not only that individuals are given access to knowledge about art, politics and biopolitics, but also that they are given this knowledge through art, through theatre, through performance. This also proves how powerful and effective a 'weapon' for aesthetic and political discussion theatre still is. The 'global', interdisciplinary support that Kurtz and the Critical Art Ensemble have received throughout 2004–5 finally shows the actual, and 'global', need for further thinking, debating, artistic performance and, perhaps most urgently, legislation on this dangerous field where art meets life, life becomes money, and politics are inevitably turned into biopolitics. Through individual cellular practice, the local can still become global and, in true Brechtian fashion, theatre can still play a major role in effecting social change.

7   Conclusion

Globalisation is a phase in the development of capitalism that affects the production of life. Not only does it enter our lives, through what we eat and drink, how we dress, dwell, work, talk and think, but it also encompasses all our discourses, from economics to medical and biotechnological sciences, from architecture to politics, art and sociology. In its complexity, globalisation at once cannibalises and surpasses post-modernism. Whereas the latter is primarily embedded in philosophical and aesthetic discourse, globalisation is also a practice of everyday life. More than a condition, it is the texture of our cells, the anomaly of our plant, animal and human nature, the informational space in which we live, culturally and geographically, our (g)locality in relation to the rest of the world. Interestingly, globalisation is achieved through performance. It depends on culturally determined performance indicators. It relies on the production, distribution and effect of information. In this sense it acts as a giant information technology factory, aiming for the production of an INFO-spectacle, which, like a magic circus, needs the constant attendance of a fair of animals and humans who at once produce, consume and witness everything around them.

Through globalisation, the becoming of life is reduced to the economic production of Life®™. Since Dolly's birth, pigs, cows, cats, horses, mice, rabbits and goats have all been cloned. Some have been produced for medical reasons, some for research and some have been created as replicas of elite animals. The possibility to make copies of pets or extinct animals, however ethically questionable, is already a reality. The cloning of a human embryo was announced on 19 May 2005 in the UK. Drugs may be tailored for specific individuals, submitted by a microchip, intravenously. Cells, proteins even, which make enzymes, hormones, 'turn cells on and off, cause us to grow and to grow old, to get sick, to heal, to get pregnant, flower, wilt, and die' (Duncan, 2001: 166), may be produced in large biotechnological factories and sold to us to affect the course of our lives. The word famine might really only just appear in history books. Lumps of meat are already directly produced in science laboratories, derived from cells, so that 'with a single cell' one could, at least theoretically, produce 'the world's annual meat supply' (Sample, 2005).

Globalisation needs to be managed, legally and politically, so that its benefits will be of true global consequence. Cultural activity must play a fundamental role within this process. Although globalisation takes place an age of biotechnological and biopolitical control, culture is still the principal means through which this control is exerted. In fact, contrary to popular belief, cloning 'does *not* offer an instant and exact replication of the original' (Wilmut in Wilmut *et al.*, 2000: 4, added emphasis). Thus, for instance, Cedric, Cecil, Cyril and Tuppence (Figure 7.1), all cloned in 1999 at the Roslin Institute from cultured embryo cells, were 'four young Dorset rams who are genetically identical to one another and yet are very different in size and temperament, showing emphatically that an animal's genes do *not* "determine" every detail of its physique and personality' (ibid.: 5, original emphasis). This suggests that, whatever form of biological control may have been used in the production of a given plant, animal, or even human being, its *environment* is still of crucial consequence to its development. This also suggests that the response to globalisation comes from within it, for globalisation encompasses radical artistic and political practices, including the anti-globalisation movement, hacktivism, urban performance practice engaging with urbanity through surveillance technologies, cyborg, robotic, prosthetic and post-human body and carnal art, A-Life- and AI-based artistic practices recreating nature and intelligence, cellular practice and even transgenic and

Figure 7.1 Cedric, Cecil, Cyril and Tuppence (source: Courtesy of the Roslin Institute).

semi-living art, which are already in the process of shaping this complex movement from within.

A crucial part of globalisation is represented by technological (g)locisation. Through surveillance technologies, we are at once watching and being watched by the world. This allows for the formation of online distributed communities, networks of people or 'smart mobs', acting in 'concert', even though they may be geographically dispersed and share nothing but a common cause. Connected by mobile devices to 'other information devices in the environment as well as with other people's telephones', smart mobs are gaining 'new forms of social power' (Rheingold, 2002: xii) so much so that, as Howard Rheingold reports, 'the People Power II smart mobs in Manila overthrew the President Estrada in 2001 through a series of demonstrations organised via text-messaging' (ibid.: xvii). Smart mobs are at once volatile and powerful, individually minded and globally effective.

Researchers in Artificial Intelligence and computational methods often adopt swarms as a way of naming collective and distributed techniques of problem solving without centralised control or the provision of a global model. Whereas previously it was assumed that intelligence resided in individuals' minds, now it appears that *intelligence is distributed and social* (see Hardt and Negri, 2000 and 2004). Eugene Thacker, who defines a swarm as 'an organization of multiple, individuated units with some relation to one another', notes that 'a swarm is a collectivity that is defined by relationality' and that 'relation is the rule in swarms'. Thacker also draws attention to the fact that 'a swarm is a whole that is more than the sum of its parts, but it is also a *heterogeneous* whole' (2004: added emphasis). Moreover, 'the principles of self-organization require that the group *only* arises from the localized, singular, heterogeneous actions of individual units' (ibid., original emphasis).

Steven Johnson's analysis of the slime mould, a very primitive organism and a close relative of ordinary fungi, throws some light on the way swarms operate. 'With no centralised brain whatsoever', Johnson notes, and spending 'much of its life as thousands of distinct single-celled units, each moving separately from its other comrades' the swarm, 'under the right conditions'

> will coalesce again into a single, larger organism, which then begins its leisurely crawl across the garden floor, consuming rotten leaves and wood as it moves about. When the environment is less hospitable, the slime mold acts as a single organism; when the weather turns cooler and the mold enjoys a large food supply, 'it' becomes a 'they'. *The slime mold oscillates between being a single creature and a swarm.*
>
> (2002: 11, added emphasis)

Likewise, 'ants – each limited to a meager vocabulary of pheromones and minimal cognitive skills – collectively engage in nuanced and improvisational problem solving'. So, for instance, a harvester ant colony in the field will not only ascertain the shortest route to a food source, it will also prioritise food sources, based on their distance and ease of access. In response to changing external conditions, worker ants switch from nest-building to foraging to raising ant pupae.

Most crucially, 'none of the individual ants is actually "in charge" of the overall operation': 'they think locally *and* act locally, but their collective action produces global behaviour' (ibid.: 74, original emphasis). The formation of swarms, or smart mobs, distributed global communities performing together towards achieving a radical act, is the means by which a geographically dispersed and culturally diverse group can directly affect and possibly even shape the course of globalisation.

As Steve Shapin and Simon Schaffer's 20-year-old ending of their seminal work, *The Leviathan and the Air Pump*, claimed, '[a]s we come to recognise the conventional and artifactual status of our forms of knowing, we put ourselves in a position to realise that it is ourselves and not reality that is responsible for what we know'. (1989: 344). Since knowledge 'is the product of human actions' (ibid.), and because 'solutions to the problem of knowledge are solutions to the problem of social order' (ibid.: 332), it is imperative that we reclaim responsibility for the world we are creating legally, politically, scientifically *and* artistically. Our culture and technology, our knowledge, is all we have got to shape our future.

Bibliography

Adams, M. (2005) interview to G. Giannachi, London, 11 April 2005, author's private archive.

Albrow, M. and King, E. (eds) (1990) *Globalization, Knowledge and Society*, London: Sage.

Anon (2002) www.telefonica.es/fat/eantunez.html (accessed 4 November 2002).

Arluke, A. and Sanders, C.R. (1996) *Regarding Animals*, Philadelphia, Pennsylvania: Temple University Press.

Armstrong, S. (2003) 'Strange Brain', *Sunday Times*, 9 June.

Ascott, R. (ed.) (2000) *Art, Technology, Consciousness: mind@large*, Bristol: Intellect.

Auslander, P. (1997) *From Acting to Performance: Essays in Modernism and Post-modernism*, London and New York: Routledge.

Badie, B. (1995) *La fin des territories: Essai sur le désordre international et sur l'utilité sociale du respect*, Paris: Fayard.

Balsamo, A. (1999; [1996]) *Technologies of the Gendered Body: Reading Cyborg Women*, Durham, North Carolina and London: University of California Press.

Baudrillard, J. (1988) *The Ecstasy of Communication*, trans. B. Schutze and C. Schutze, New York: Semiotext(e).

—— (1995; [1991]) *The Gulf War Did Not Take Place*, trans. Power Institute and P. Patton, Sydney: Power Publications.

—— (1995a) 'The Virtual Illusion or the Automatic Writing of the World', *Theory, Culture and Society*, 12: 97–107.

—— (2003) 'The Violence of the Global', CTHEORY, A129 (20 May). Online. Available at: www.ctheory.net/home.aspx (accessed 3 June 2003).

Bauman, Z. (1998) *Globalization, the Human Consequences*, Cambridge: Polity Press.

Baumgärtel, T. (2001) *{net.art 2.0} Neue Materiale zur Netzkunst/New Materials Towards Net Art*, Nürnberg: Verlag für moderne Kunst.

Beck, U. (2000) *What Is Globalization?*, trans. P. Camiller, Cambridge: Polity Press.

Beckmann, J. (1998) *The Virtual Dimension*, New York: Princeton Architectural Press.

Bell, D. and Kennedy, B. (eds) (2000) *The Cybercultures Reader*, London and New York: Routledge.

Bender, G. and Druckrey, T. (1994) *Culture on the Brink: Ideologies of Technology*, Seattle, Washington: Bay Press.

Benthien, C. (2002; [1999]) *Skin: on the Cultural Border between Self and the World*, trans. T. Dunlap, New York: Columbia University Press.

Biological Resource Management in Agriculture (2004) 'Challenges and Risks of Genetically Engineered Organisms', OECD, LSE archive.

Blast Theory (1998) *Kidnap*, DVD, company archive.

—— (2000) 'Desert Rain'. Online. Available at: www.blastheory.easynet.co.uk/ work_desertrain_desc_body.html (accessed 8 December 2000).

—— (2002) *Desert Rain*, catalogue, company archive.

—— (2005) Blast Theory. Online. Available at: www.blastheory (accessed 1 March 2005).

Boyer, M.C. (1994) *The City of Collective Memory: Its Historical Imagery and Architectural Enhancements*, Cambridge, Massachusetts: MIT Press.

—— (1996) *Cybercities: Visual Perception in the Age of Electronic Communication*, New York: Princeton Architectural.

Butler, J. (1990) *Gender Trouble*, London and New York: Routledge.

Canguilhem, G. (1978) *On the Normal and the Pathological*, trans. C.R. Fawcett, Boston, Massachusetts: Reidel.

Carter, M. (1995) 'Guerrilla Programming of Video Surveillance Equipment'. Online. Available at: www.notbored.org/gpvse.html (accessed 18 April 2005).

Castells, M. (1989) *The Informational City: Information Technology, Economic Restructuring, and the Urban-Regional Process*, Oxford: Basil Blackwell.

—— (1997) *The Power of Identity. The Information Age: Economy, Society and Culture*, Vol. I, Oxford: Blackwell.

Catts, O. and Zurr, I. (2002) 'Growing Semi-Living Sculptures: The Tissue Culture and Art Project', *Leonardo*, 35: 4, 365–70.

Cavallaro, D. (2000) *Cyberpunk and Cyberculture*, London: Athlone Press.

Chase-Dunn, C., Kawano, Y. and Brewer, B. (2000) 'Trade Globalization since 1795: Waves of Integration in the World-System', *American Sociological Review*, 65, 77–95.

Churcher, N. (2003) 'Blast Masters', *Design Week*, 29 May, 19.

Clark, D. (1996) *Urban World/Global City*, London and New York: Routledge.

Clarke, R. (2001) 'Reigning Territorial Plains – Blast Theory's "Desert Rain"', *Performance Research*, 6: 2, 43–50.

Connor, S. (2005) 'Word First: Brain Cells Grown in Laboratory', *The Independent*, 14 June.

Conrad, P. and Gabe, J. (eds) (1999) *Sociological Perspectives on the New Genetics*, Oxford: Blackwell.

Crang, M., Crang, Ph. and May, J. (1999) *Virtual Geographies: Bodies, Space and Relations*, London and New York: Routledge.

Critical Art Ensemble (1995) *The Mythology of Terrorism on the Net*. Online. Available at: www.t0.or.at/cae/mnterror.htm (accessed 13 June 2003).

—— (1996) *Electronic Civil Disobedience*. Online. Available at: www.critical-art.net (accessed 6 May 2003).

—— (1998) *Flesh Machine*. Online. Available at: www.critical-art.net (accessed 6 May 2003).

—— (2002) *The Molecular Invasion*. Online. Available at: www.critical-art.net (accessed 6 May 2003).

—— (2003) *Posthuman Development in the Age of Pancapitalism*. Online. Available at: t0.or.at/cae/psthuman.htm (accessed 13 June 2003).

—— (2004) *BioCom*. Online. Available at: www.critical-art.net/biotech/biocom/ biocomWeb/product.html (accessed 5 March 2004).

—— (2004a) *Society for Reproductive Anachronisms*. Online. Available at: www.critical-art.net/biotech/sra/index.html (accessed 5 March 2004).

—— (2004b) *GenTerra*. Online. Available at: www.critical-art.net/biotech/gen-terra/index/html (accessed 5 March 2004).

—— (2004c) Critical Art Ensemble Defense Fund. Online. Available at: www.caedefensefund.org/ (accessed 4 October 2005).

Cross, M. and Moore, R. (eds) (2002) *Globalisation and the New City: Migrants, Minorities and Urban Transformations in Comparative Perspective*, Houndmills: Palgrave.

Debord, G. (1995 [1967]) *The Society of the Spectacle*, trans. D. Nicholson-Smith, New York: Zone Books.

Deleuze, G. and Guattari, F. (1999; [1980]) *A Thousand Plateaus: Capitalism and Schizophrenia*, trans. B. Massumi, London: Athlone Press.

Dery, M. (1996) *Escape Velocity*, London: Hodder and Stoughton.

Donaldson, L. Sir and May, Sir R. (1999) 'Health Implications of Genetically Modified Foods', House of Commons Science and Technology Committee, LSE archive.

Duncan, D. (2001) 'The Protein Hunters', *Wired*, 4: 164–71.

Eco, U. (1964) *Apocalittici e Integrati*, Milan: Bompiani.

Editorial (2004) 'Why Scientists Should Support an Artist in Trouble?' *Nature*, 17 June, 429, 685.

—— (2005) 'Beyond the Yuck Factor', *New Scientist*, 25 June, 5.

etoy (2004) etoy. Online. Available at: www.etoy.com/ (accessed 15 January 2005).

Featherstone, M. (1982) 'The Body in Consumer Culture', *Theory, Culture and Society*, 1, 18–33.

—— (ed.) (2000) *Body Modification*, London: Sage.

Featherstone, M. and Burrows, R. (1995) *Cyberspace, Cyberbodies, Cyberpunk*, London: Sage.

Featherstone M. and Lash, S. (1995) 'Globalisation, Modernity and the Spatialisation of Social Theory: An Introduction', in M. Featherstone, S. Lash and R. Robertson (eds) *Global Modernities*, London: Sage.

Featherstone, M., Lash, S. and Robertson, R. (eds) (1997; [1995]) *Global Modernities*, London: Sage.

Fleming, C. (2002) 'Performance as Guerrilla Ontology: The Case of Stelarc', *Body & Society*, 8:3, 95–109.

Foucault, M. (1991; [1975]) *Discipline and Punish: The Birth of the Prison*, trans. A. Sheridan, Harmondsworth: Penguin.

Franklin, S. (1998) 'Animal Models: An Anthropologist Considers Dolly'. Online. Available at: www.comp.lancs.ac.uk/sociology/soc048sf.html (accessed 30 April 2003).

—— (2003) 'Life Itself: Global Nature and the Genetic Imaginary'. Online. Available at: www.comp.lancs.ac.uk/sociology/soc048sf.html (accessed 30 April 2003).

Franklin, S. and Lock, M. (eds) (2003) *Remaking Life & Death: Towards an Anthropology of the Biosciences*, Santa Fe, New Mexico: School of American Research Press.

Franklin, S., Lury, C. and Stacey, J. (2000) *Global Nature, Global Culture*, London: Sage.

Fraser, M. and Greco, M. (2005) *The Body: A Reader*, London and New York: Routledge.

Frauenfelder, M. (1998) 'Do-It-Yourself Darwin: Karl Sims Invites You to Play God among machines'. Online. Available at: www.wired.com/wired/archive/6.10/sims_pr.html (30 April 2003).

Fu-Chen Lo and Yue-Man Yeung (eds) (1998) *Globalisation and the World of Large Cities*, Tokyo, New York, Paris: United Nations University Press.

Fukuyama, F. (1992) *The End of History and the Last Man*, New York: Free Press.

—— (2002) *Our Posthuman Future: Consequences of the Biotechnology Revolution*, London: Profile Books.

Fusco, C. (2003) 'On-Line Simulations/Real-Life Politics: A Discussion with Ricardo Dominguez on Staging Virtual Theatre', *The Drama Review*, T178, 47: 2, 151–62.

Genewatch UK (2000) 'Privatising Knowledge, Patenting Genes: The Race to Control Genetic Information', Briefing Number 11, June, LSE archive.

Giannachi, G. (2004) *Virtual Theatres, an Introduction*, London and New York: Routledge.

Giannachi, G. and Kaye, N. (2002) *Staging the Post-Avant-Garde: Italian Experimental Performance after 1970*, Oxford, Bern and New York: Peter Lang.

Giannachi, G. and Stewart, N. (2005) *Performing Nature: Explorations in Ecology and the Arts*, Oxford, Bern and New York: Peter Lang.

Giannetti, C. (ed.) (1998) *Marcel·lì Antúnez Roca: Performances, objetos y dibujos*, Disseny: MECAD, Media Centre d'Art.

Giannetti, C. (ed.) (1999) *Marcel·lì Antúnez Roca: Epifanía*, Madrid: Fundación Telefónica.

Giddens, A. (1990) *The Consequences of Modernity*, Cambridge: Polity Press.

—— (2000) *The Third Way and Its Critics*, Cambridge: Polity Press.

Goldberg, K. (ed.) (2000) *The Robot in the Garden: Telerobotics and Telepistemology in the Age of the Internet*, Cambridge, Massachusetts: MIT Press.

Goodman, A., Heath, D. and Lindee, M.S. (2003) *Genetic Nature/Culture: Anthropology and Science beyond the Two-Culture Divide*, Berkeley, Los Angeles and London: University of California Press.

Graham, E.L. (2002) *Representations of the Post/human: Monsters, Aliens and Others in Popular Culture*, Manchester: Manchester University Press.

Grand, S. (2003) 'Steve Grand: Cyberlife'. Online. Available at: www.cyberlife-research.com/people/steve/ (accessed 20 May 2003).

Grau, O. (2003) *Virtual Art: from Illusion to Immersion*, Cambridge, Massachusetts and London: MIT Press.

Gray, C.H. (ed.) (1995) *The Cyborg Handbook*, London and New York: Routledge.

—— (2001) *Cyborg Citizen: Politics in the Posthuman Age*, London and New York: Routledge.

Greene, R. (2004) *Internet Art*, London and New York: Thames and Hudson.

Grzinic, M. (2002) *Stelarc*, Ljubljana, Maribor: Maska MKC.

Gustafson, M. (2000) 'The Tattoo in the Later Roman Empire and Beyond', in J. Caplan (ed.) *Written on the Body: The Tattoo in European and American History*, Princeton, New Jersey: Princeton University Press.

Hall, P. (1966; second edn) *The World Cities*, London: Weidenfeld and Nicolson.

Hamilton, B. (2004) 'Hidden Eyes of Our Apple: Or the Return of Howard Safir', *The New York Post*, 2 May, also online. Available at: www.notbored.org/safir-returns.html (accessed 18 April 2005).

Haraway, D. (1991) *Simians, Cyborgs, and Women: The Reinvention of Nature*, London: Free Association Books.

—— (1997) Modest_Witness@Second_Millennium: FemaleMan©_Meets_Oncomouse™, London and New York: Routledge.

Hardt, M. and Negri, A. (2000) *Empire*, Cambridge, Massachusetts and London: Harvard University Press.

—— (2004) *Multitude: War and Democracy in the Age of Empire*, New York: Penguin Press.

Hayles, K. (1999) *How We Became Posthuman: Virtual Bodies in Cybernetics, Literature, and Informatics*, Chicago and London: University of Chicago Press.

Heathfield, A. (2003) *Live: Art and Performance*, London: Tate Publishing.

Heller, A. and Puntscher Riekmann, S. (eds) (1996) *Biopolitics. The Politics of the Body, Race and Nature*, Aldershot: Avebury.

Holmes, D. (ed.) (2001) *Virtual Globalisation: Virtual Spaces/Tourist Spaces*, London and New York: Routledge.

Hübler, K. (1997) 'Knowbotic Research: Non-located Events: Interventions between the Urban and the Electronic Environment'. Online. Available at: www.canon.co.jp/cast/artlab/artlab7/lecture2.html (accessed 6 January 2003).

Imperiale, A. (2000) *New Flatness, Surface Tension in Digital Architecture*, Basel: Birkhäuser.

Ince, K. (2000) *Orlan: Millennial Female*, Oxford and New York: Berg.

Jameson, F. (1991) *Postmodernism, or, The Cultural Logic of Late Capitalism*, London and New York: Verso.

Johnson, S. (2002) *Emergence: the Connected Lives of Ants, Brains, Cities and Software*, London: Penguin.

Kac, E. (2002) Eduardo Kac. Online. Available at: www.ekac.org (accessed 2 December 2002).

Karakotsios, K. (1993) 'The New Frontier'. Online. Available at: www.aec.at/en/archiv_files/19931/E1993_109.html (accessed 12 May 2003).

Kay, L.E. (2000) *Who Wrote the Book of Life? A History of Genetic Code*, Stanford, California: Stanford University Press.

Kaye, N. (2000) *Site-Specific Art: Performance, Place and Documentation*, London and New York: Routledge.

Kember, S. (2003) *Cyberfeminism and Artificial Life*, London and New York: Routledge.

Kemp, S. (2004) *Future Face: Image, Identity, Innovation*, London: Profile Books.

King, A. (1990) *Global Cities: Post-Imperialism and the Internationalisation of London*, London: Routledge.

Kostic, A. and Dobrila, P.T. (eds) (2000) *Eduardo Kac: Telepresence, Biotelematics, Transgenetic Art*, Ljubljana: Publication of the Association for Culture and Education.

Lane, J. (2003) 'Digital Zapatistas', *Modern Drama*, T178, 47: 2, 129–44.

Langton, C. (ed.) (1989) *Artificial Life*, Redwood City, California: Addison-Wesley.

Lash, S. and Urry, J. (1987) *The End of Organised Capitalism*, Cambridge: Polity Press.

—— (1994) *Economies of Signs and Space*, London: Sage.

Latour, B. (2004) *Politics of Nature: How to Bring the Sciences into Democracy*, trans. C. Porter, Cambridge, Massachusetts and London: Harvard University Press.

Leeker, M. (ed.) (2001) *Maschinen, Medien, Performances: Theater and der Schnittstelle zu digitalen Welten*, Berlin: Alexander Verlag.

Lenoir, T. (2002) 'Makeover: Writing the Body into the Posthuman Technoscape: Part One: Embracing the Posthuman', *Configurations*, 10: 2, 203–20.

Lunenfeld, P. (2001; third edn) *The Digital Dialectic*, Cambridge, Massachusetts: MIT Press.

Lury, C. (2004) *Brands: The Logos of the Global Economy*, London and New York: Routledge.

Lyon, D. (2001) *Surveillance Society: Monitoring Everyday Life*, Buckingham, Pennsylvania: Open University Press.

Lyon, D. and Zureik, E. (eds) (1996) *Computers, Surveillance, and Privacy*, Minneapolis and London: University of Minnesota Press.

McCarthy, P. (1983) 'The Body Obsolete: Stelarc and Paul McCarthy Talk about the Power the Body Has over Itself', *High Performance*, 24: 14–19.

McKenzie, J. (2001) *Perform or Else: From Discipline to Performance*, London and New York: Routledge.

Mackintosh, H. (2001) 'I Robot: Interview with Professor Kevin Warwick, 4 October. Online. Available at: www.guardian.co.uk/Archive/Article/0,4273, 4269537,00.html (accessed 12 May 2005).

Macnaghten, P. and Urry, J. (1998) *Contested Nature*, London: Sage Publications.

—— (eds) (2001) *Bodies of Nature*, London: Sage Publications.

Mann, S. (1997) 'Wearable Computing: A First Step towards Personal Imaging', *Cybersquare*, 30:2. Online. Available at: www.wearcam.org/ieeecomputer/ r2025.htm (accessed 19 August 2005).

Manovich, L. (2001) *The Language of New Media*, Cambridge, Massachusetts: MIT Press.

Masood, E. (1998) 'Pressure grows for inquiry into welfare of transgenic animals', *Nature*, 24 July, 388: 311–12.

Meikle, G. (2002) *Future Active: Media Activism and the Internet*, London and New York: Routledge.

Mitchell, R. and Thurtle, P. (eds) (2004) *Data Made Flesh: Embodying Information*, London and New York: Routledge.

Morgan, K.P. (1991) 'Women and the Knife: Cosmetic Surgery and the Colonization of Women's Bodies', *Hypathia*, 6: 25–53.

Mulder, A. and Post, M. (2000) *Book for the Electronic Arts*, Rotterdam: De Balie.

Negri, A. (2003) *Guide: Cinque lezioni su impero e dintorni*, Milan: Raffaello Cortina Editore.

Noske, B. (1989) *Humans and Other Animals: Beyond the Boundaries of Anthropology*, London: Pluto Press.

Orlans, B.F. (1993) *In the Name of Science, Issues in Responsible Animal Experimentation*, New York and Oxford: Oxford University Press.

Phelan, P. (1993) *Unmarked: The Politics of Performance*, New York and London: Routledge.

Phelan, P. and Lane, J. (eds) (1998) *The Ends of Performance*, New York and London: New York University Press.

Poster, M. (1995) *The Second Media Age*, Cambridge: Polity Press.

®TMark (2005) ®TMark. Online. Available at: www.rtmark.com/ (accessed 25 January 2005).

Rabinow, P. (1996) *Making PCR: A Story of Biotechnology*, Chicago, Illinois: Chicago University Press.

Ramesh, R. (2004) 'Monsanto's Chapatti Patent Raises Indian Ire', *The Guardian*, 31 January.

Ray, T. (2003) 'What Tierra is'. Online. Available at: www.ids.atr.co.jp/~ray/tierra/ whatis.html (accessed 30 April 2003).

Reiss, M.J. and Straughan, R. (2002; [1996]) *Improving Nature? The Science and Ethics of Genetic Engineering*, Cambridge: Cambridge University Press.

Renton, D. (ed.) (2001) *Marx on Globalisation*, London: Lawrence & Wishart.

Rheingold, H. (2002) *Smart Mobs: The Next Social Revolution*, Cambridge, Massachusetts: Perseus Publishing.

Rifkin, J. (1998) *The Biotech Century: Harnessing the Gene and Remaking the World*, London: Victor Gollancz.

Robertson, G, Mash, N., Tickner, L., Bird, J., Curtis, B. and Putnam, T. (1996) *Futurenatural: Nature/science/culture*, London and New York: Routledge.

Roslin Institute (1998) Roslin Institute. Online. Available at: www.roslin.ac.uk/ (accessed 1 July 2005).

Rothman, D.J., Rose, E., Awaya, T., Cohen, B., Daar, A., Dzemeshkevich, S.L., Lee, C.J., Munro, R., Reyes, H., Rothman, S.M., Schoen, K.F., Scheper-Hughes, N., Shapira, Z. and Smit, H. (1997) 'The Bellagio Task Force Report on Transplantation, Bodily Integrity and the International Traffic in Organs', *Transplantation Proceedings*, 29, 2739–45, also online. Available at: www.icrc.org/Web/Eng/ siteeng0.nsf/iwpList302/87DC95FCA3C3D63EC1256B66005B3F6C (accessed 5 May 2005).

Sample, I. (2005) 'When Meat Is Not Murder', *Guardian*, 13 August.

Sassen, S. (1991) *The Global City: New York, London, Tokyo*, Princeton, New Jersey: Princeton University Press.

—— (2000) *Cities in a World Economy*, Thousand Oaks, California and London: Pine Forge Press.

—— (2001; second edn) *The Global City: New York, London, Tokyo*, Princeton, New Jersey: Princeton University Press.

—— (2002) *Global Networks, Linked Cities*, London and New York: Routledge.

Scheper-Hughes, N. and Wacquant, L. (eds) (2002) *Commodifying Bodies*, London: Sage.

Schneider, R. (2000) 'Nomadmedia: On Critical Art Ensemble', *TDR*, 44: 4, 120–31.

Shanken, E. (1998) 'Life as We Know It and/or Life as It Could Be', *Leonardo*, 31: 5, 383–8.

Shapin, S. and Schaffer, S. (1989; [1985]) *Leviathan and the Air Pump: Hobbes, Boyle, and the Experimental Life*, Princeton, New Jersey: Princeton University Press.

Shilling, C. (2003; [1993]) *The Body and Social Theory*, London: Sage.

Shiva, V. and Moser, I. (1995) *Biopolitics: A Feminist and Ecological Reader on Biotechnology*, London: Zed Books.

Simmonds, R. and Hack, G. (eds) (2000) *Global City Regions, Their Emerging Forms*, London and New York: Spon Press.

Slack, J. (2005) Email correspondence with G. Giannachi (dated 1 and 4 July 2005), author's private archive.

Sommerer, C. and Mignonneau, L. (eds) (1998) *Art @ Science*, Vienna and New York: Springer.

—— (1999) 'Art as a Living System: Interactive Computer Artworks', *Leonardo*, 32:3, 165–73.

—— (2000) Christa Sommerer and Laurent Mignonneau. Online. Available at: www.mic.atr.co.jp/~christa> (accessed 6 December 2000).

Sorkin, M. (1992) *Variations on a Theme Park: The New American City and the End of Public Space*, Cambridge, Massachusetts: Blackwell.

Stelarc (1997) 'From Psycho to Cyber Strategies: Prosthetics, Robotics and Remote Experience', *Cultural Values*, 1: 2, 241–9.

—— (2002) Stelarc. Online. Available at: www.stelarc.va.com.au (accessed 12 April 2002).

—— (2002a) interview with G. Giannachi, Lancaster, 10 May 2002, author's archive.

—— (2005) Stelarc. Online. Available at: www.stelarc.va.com.au/quarterear/ (accessed 24 September 2005).

Stocker, G. and Schöpf, C. (eds) (1998) *InfoWar: Ars Electronica 1998*, Vienna and New York: Springer Verlag.

—— (eds) (1999) *Life Science: Ars Electronica 1999*, Vienna and New York: Springer Verlag.

Surveillance Camera Players (1999) 'SCO Headline News'. Online. Available at: www.notbored.org/29aug99.html (accessed 18 April 2005).

—— (2005) 'How to Stage Your Own "Surveillance Camera Theater"'. Online. Available at: www.notbored.org/scp-how-to.html (accessed 18 April 2005).

SymbioticA (2005) SymbioticA. Online. Available at: www.symbiotica.uwa.edu.au/ info/info.html (accessed 21 September 2005).

Szerszynski, B., Heim W. and Waterton, C. (eds) (2003) *Nature Performed: Environment, Culture and Performance*, Oxford: Blackwell/Sociological Review.

Tester, K. (1991) *Animals and Society: The Humanity of Animal Rights*, London and New York: Routledge.

Thacker, E. (2004) 'Networks, Swarms, Multitudes', *CTHEORY*, 18 May. Online. Available at: www.ctheory.net/home.aspx (accessed 15 September 2005).

—— (2005) *The Global Genome: Biotechnology, Politics, and Culture*, Cambridge, Massachusetts and London: MIT Press.

Turner, B.S. (1992) *Regulating Bodies: Essays in Medical Sociology*, London and New York: Routledge.

Uncaged Campaign (2005) Uncaged Campaign. Online. Available at: www.uncaged.co.uk/xeno.htm#two (accessed 30 June 2005).

Unger, M. (1999) 'Taking over the Joystick of Natural Selection'. Online. Available at: www.web.genarts.com/galapagos/nyt-unger99.html (accessed 30 April 2003).

Urry, J. (2003) *Global Complexity*, Cambridge: Polity Press.

V2 (1997) *Technomorphica*, Rotterdam: V2.

—— (1998) *The Art of the Accident*, Rotterdam: Naj Publication.

Valentine, G. (2002) 'In-corporations: Food, Bodies and Organizations', *Body & Society*, 8: 2, 1–20.

van de Donk, W., Loader, B.D., Nixon, P.G. and Rucht, D. (2004) *Cyberprotest: New Media, Citizens and Social Movements*, London and New York: Routledge.

Venturi, R., Scott Brown, D. and Izenour, S. (1972) *Learning from Las Vegas: The Forgotten Symbolism of Architectural Form*, Cambridge, Massachusetts: MIT Press.

Viel, M. and Viel, R. (2005) London Centre for Aesthetic Surgery. Online. Available at: www.lcas.com/background.html (accessed 15 July 2005).

Wadman, M. (1997) 'Clinton Sketches out in His "Ethical Guideposts" for Modern Biology', *Nature*, 387, 323.

Wark, M. (2004) *A Hacker Manifesto*, Cambridge, Massachusetts and London: Harvard University Press.

Warwick, K. (2005), Kevin Warwick. Online. Available at: www.kevinwarwick.org/ (accessed 15 June 2005).

Weibel, P. and Druckrey, T. (eds) (2001) *net_condition: art and global media*, Cambridge, Massachusetts: MIT Press.

Weibel, P. and Schmid, C. (eds) (2000) *Internationaler Medien/Kunstpresse*, Karlsruhe: ZKM.

Wiener, N. (1948) *Cybernetics: or Control and Communication in the Animal and the Machine*, New York: John Wiley.

Wilmut, I., Campbell, K. and Tudge, C. (2000) *The Second Creation: Dolly and the Age of Biological Control*, Cambridge, Massachusetts: Harvard University Press.

Wilson, S.W. (1991) 'The animat path to AI', in J.-A. Meyer and S. Wilson (eds) *From Animals to Animats*, Cambridge, Massachusetts: MIT Press, pp. 15–21.

Wilson, S. (2002) *Information Arts: Intersections of Art, Science, and Technology*, Cambridge, Massachusetts: MIT Press.

The Yes Men (2005) The Yes Men. Online. Available at: www.theyesmen.org/ (accessed 15 October 2005).

Yoxen, E. (1981) 'Life as a Productive Force: Capitalizing the Science and Technology of Molecular Biology', in L. Levidow and R. Young (eds) *Science, Technology and the Labour Process*, London: Free Association Books, pp. 66–122.

Zellner, P. (1999) *Hybrid Space: New Forms in Digital Architecture*, London: Thames and Hudson.

0100101110101101.ORG (2002) 0100101110101101.ORG. Online. Available at: www.0100101110101101.org/home/gui/about.html (accessed 17 September 2002).

Zylinska, J. (2002) *The Cyborg Experiments: The Extensions of the Body in the Media Age*, London and New York: Continuum.

Index